Presented to

_____

From

_____

Date

_____

TODAY'S THE DAY

TODAY'S THE DAY

JIM STOVALL

David C Cook®

transforming lives together

TODAY'S THE DAY
Published by David C. Cook
4050 Lee Vance View
Colorado Springs, CO 80918 U.S.A.

David C. Cook Distribution Canada
55 Woodslee Avenue, Paris, Ontario, Canada N3L 3E5

David C. Cook U.K., Kingsway Communications
Eastbourne, East Sussex BN23 6NT, England

David C. Cook and the graphic circle C logo
are registered trademarks of Cook Communications Ministries.

The Web site addresses recommended throughout this book are offered as a resource to
you. These Web sites are not intended in any way to be or imply an endorsement on the
part of David C. Cook, nor do we vouch for their content.

LCCN 2007933214
ISBN 978-0-7814-4845-1

© 2007 Jim Stovall

Cover Design: BMB Design, Inc.

Printed in United States of America
First Edition 2007

2 3 4 5 6 7 8 9 10 11 12

101207

This book is dedicated to two people who have made my pursuit of being a columnist possible. First, Ralph Schaefer, Business Journal editor, who encouraged me to write a single article and then told me to just do it every week, and I would be a columnist. And, last but never least, this book is also dedicated to my friend and colleague Dorothy Thompson, without whom none of my readers would ever have heard of me.

A s a blind person, I live in a different world than those of you reading the words on this page; however, that doesn't mean that I don't "see." Several years ago I recognized a universal ritual among most sighted people—that of reading a daily newspaper. Most busy individuals find a few moments in their hectic day to scan one or more sections of a local, regional, or national publication.

But most newspapers are filled with horrific headlines, terrifying financial information, and obligatory obituaries. What if this daily ritual happened to include a small dose of goodness? Several years ago I began writing a regularly syndicated column entitled "Winners' Wisdom" to try to bring a little fresh air to these few moments most everyone shares.

The world we live in is made up of all kinds of people, but everyone ultimately falls into one of two categories when measuring success: winners or losers. I want to be a winner. And I believe you do too. So I've compiled ninety of the "Winners' Wisdom" columns I've written and placed them in this book, *Today's the Day*.

Each entry is short; I'm just trying to add a little fresh air to the day. But short doesn't mean shallow. I hope you will read these reflections as invitations to see and do: an invitation to "see" the wisdom I've seen and an invitation to act on it in your own life. And become a winner!

Today's the day!

Most of us work very hard. We get up each day and spend eight hours or more doing something we call work. If you talk to the most successful and the least successful persons you can find, they will probably tell you they are working extremely hard. If this is true, why are so few people actually getting the results they want from their hard work?

Quite simply, they confuse activity with productivity. Just because you're doing something doesn't mean you're really getting anywhere. We have all seen hamsters running around on the little wheel in their cage. They create a tremendous amount of activity but no productivity.

Recently, I did some consulting for a sales organization. These sales people work solely on commission, so the only productive thing they really do is talk to new people about their products and services. Before our training session, the average salesperson told me they were working very hard for eight to ten hours every day. Once they learned that their only productive task was talking to new people about their products or services, we conducted a simple experiment. Each salesperson was given a stopwatch and instructed to keep it in their pocket and click it on only when they were talking to a new prospect, either on the telephone or in person. We discovered that the top wage earners were actually productive only three hours per day. The average and below-average producers were far less productive.

If you want to be more successful, earn more, or reach your goals faster, simply separate activity from productivity and commit at least half of your workday to productivity. The difference will amaze you. Your destiny awaits.

Today's the day!

The Wisdom of the Snapping Turtle

When I was eight years old, during one of my journeys into the woods, I successfully captured a rather large snapping turtle. I immediately brought him back to my grandparents' house, selected an appropriate box, and made him my official pet. Because I was being particularly quiet, my grandfather came onto the back porch to determine what mischief I might be pursuing. I showed him my prize turtle and explained that it was now my pet.

My grandfather took a pencil out of his shirt pocket and poked the turtle under his shell until he extended his head and promptly bit the end of the pencil completely off. Then my grandfather turned to me and asked me a question that remains with me even today. He asked, "Now that you know what your turtle can do, if you stick your finger in there and he bites it off, is it your fault or his?"

As an eight-year-old, this was very simple. I knew that if I allowed my turtle to bite off my finger, it would be my fault. I am very pleased to inform you that as of this writing, I am still in possession of all ten fingers.

Many of us as adults forget the wisdom of the turtle, and we get bitten time after time. We don't fail because we don't know what to do. We fail because we don't do what we know. Sigmund Freud said that insanity is defined as doing the same thing over and over but continually expecting a different result. If you keep sticking your fingers in the turtle's mouth, you will continue to lose fingers. If you want a different result in your life, take a different action. Starting now.

Today's the day!

All of us had wonderful dreams, goals, and plans when we were teenagers or young adults. But at some point reality sets in, and we let our dreams and goals slip further and further back into our minds. We actually ship all of our dreams and goals to a mythical place I call "Someday Isle."

"Someday Isle" is a picture-postcard kind of place where the weather is always perfect, and everything is always wonderful—except nothing ever happens. And now, every time we think of those long-forgotten dreams and goals, we say to ourselves, "Someday, I'll do this; someday, I'll do that." But someday never comes.

General George Patton said that a good plan violently executed now, is better than a perfect plan next week. This applies to each of us as we go through our lives. Please remember that the biggest dream you ever had in your life is still alive and well. It will return to you from "Someday Isle" as soon as you make it a priority in your present-day life.

Your destiny is too wonderful to delay any longer. Make the commitment. Take the steps. Pay the price.

Today's the day!

In our society, we revere those who are the best at what they do. Chants of "We're number one!" are heard frequently. You will never hear, "We're number two," or "We're not great, but we're better than we were last year." If we want to be the best at whatever we do, we have to break it down into its individual components.

"B" is for Balance. It is the element that keeps our lives stable. We've all heard about superstar athletes, multimillionaires, and movie stars who wreck their health or family relationships in their quest for greatness. No matter how much we achieve in one area of our life, if we lose the overall perspective that we are multifaceted beings, we can never be successful.

"E" is for Enthusiasm. This is the first thing we receive when we enter this world as the doctor slaps us on the backside, and it is the last thing we give up before they close the coffin lid. I have had the privilege of interviewing superstars from the worlds of entertainment, sports, and politics, and the one thing that each of these individuals has in common is a tremendous passion and enthusiasm for what he or she does. If you don't feel that kind of daily passion as you pursue your life goals, you need to get either a new career or a new attitude about the career you are currently pursuing.

"S" is for Single-mindedness. This is the ability to focus on one thing at a time. This does not mean we are one-dimensional in our lives. It simply means, when we are working, we work; when we are playing, we play. And any other task we choose to undertake receives our total attention and focus.

"T" is for Tenacity. This is the one element that will always result in eventual success. As a blind person, I could hit a baseball thrown by the best pitcher in the major league if you would let me keep trying until I succeed. The immortal message from Winston Churchill echoes down through the years: "never give in, never give in, never, never, never...."

Go out and be the B.E.S.T.

Today's the day!

B y now, you may have noticed that each column ends with the phrase "Today's the day!" This is not an accident.

A sense of urgency is the most vital element in your success. There are many great ideas that never amount to anything more than a great idea because we fail to take that all-important first step.

Recently, I have been dealing with the imminent death of a close family member. This creates a new and very valuable perspective. I have been experiencing a sense of immediacy in that I want to say and do important things before it's too late. In reality, we should all live our lives this way.

In business terms, yesterday is a canceled check that is of no value, and tomorrow is a promissory note that may or may not be any good. The only real currency that we can spend is today. If you have a dream, a goal, or an objective that is worthy of your attention and consideration, I believe that it is a gift that has been given to you. With that gift, there is a responsibility to act upon it—not someday or tomorrow but today.

I believe that for every goal in our lives, there is a step that can be taken today. Maybe it is simply studying and learning, preparation, or meeting new people who can help us along the way. It's important to have lifelong objectives and long-term goals, but remember they don't mean anything unless we embrace the eternal truth that when you boil life down to its essence, *now* is the only thing that really matters.

Today's the day!

A Disease Called More

Years of success and prosperity in our economy have created a consumer-based society. We are no longer worried about our physical or financial survival; therefore, we have undertaken a new challenge. As a people, we have embraced the illusive challenge of accumulating more. Please understand that there is absolutely nothing wrong with enjoying material possessions. It is important, however, to draw a distinction between the possessions we have and those possessions that have us.

If your goal is to acquire a certain standard of living or lifestyle for you and your family or for your future security, that ambition is admirable. However, if it is your burning desire to keep up with the image portrayed by the commercials on television or in the glamour magazines, you have been afflicted with the dreaded disease called "more."

More is a disease that feeds upon itself like a thirst that can never be quenched. As we rush about aimlessly trying to accumulate more, we become aware of an even greater number of things we don't have and must obtain. Instead of seeking the impossible goal of reaching more, we should seek the internal goal that is called "enough."

Ironically, we can find people who literally are billionaires and who have long ago lost count of all of their possessions. However, these people are still driven on that eternal quest for more. On the other hand, there are people of seemingly modest means who have attained the admirable state of enough. They no longer judge themselves based on what they have, but instead, on who they are. They have come to the conclusion that it is more important to be someone special than to have a vast accumulation of possessions. They have reached a state of being where they understand that it is not important to be a "human having." It is only important to arrive as a "human being."

In the final analysis, many times reaching the state of enough will give you the confidence and peace of mind to be an even better person who will attract more success, resulting in the tangible possessions that have become such an addiction in our society. Focus on who you are, and allow what you have to become a result of your personal success.

Today's the day!

S uccess in life, both personally and professionally, is dependent upon our ability to successfully interact with the people around us. There is no success without positive relationships in our lives. A successful relationship is not a relationship without conflict. There is no such thing as a relationship without conflict; therefore, a successful relationship is one in which conflict is resolved.

Too many people make the mistake in their personal or professional lives of avoiding conflicts and simply not dealing with them. While in the short term, this tactic may result in a brief period of peace, the reality is that the conflict continues to build to an unmanageable point until it explodes, often making a resolution at that point impossible.

The solution to this is quite simple: Deal with all conflicts the day they arise.

My wife and I have had a policy for many years that has served us well. We deal with any potential conflict immediately. If a problem is not dealt with the day it arises, it is considered out-of-bounds at the end of the day. This forces you to either let the situation go or deal with the conflict immediately before it multiplies into something unmanageable.

We have all been in situations where someone irrationally explodes over the most minor situation. In their mind, it is not a minor situation because they are dealing with a massive pile of issues that they have let accumulate over weeks, months, or even years. Then the proverbial straw breaks the camel's back and irreparable damage is done to that relationship.

Ancient wisdom teaches us, "Don't let the sun go down on your anger." Either release it or deal with it while it's a minor issue, and every day you will start out with a clean slate in dealing with people in your personal and professional life.

Today's the day!

FOCUS

Focus is the key to turning energy into productivity. It turns our dreams into goals into reality.

On an extremely hot day, the sun will beat down with enough intensity to give you a very severe sunburn. But that's about it. That same energy when captured and concentrated in a magnifying glass can create an intense white-hot flame that can be put to any use or task you would choose.

In business today, there exists a trendy school of thought called "line extension." This theory tells us that if you have a successful company that has made a name for itself manufacturing snow tires, you should be able to take your name and attach it to other products and experience the same degree of success, thereby extending your line. While this occasionally works, it is more often a well-thought-out expansion plan, not just relabeling another product with an expectation of re-creating former success.

Companies or individuals who achieve world-class success in any area focus intensely on that area. Too often, the line extension mentality is simply a cop-out when the going gets tough, and the grass appears greener in some other pasture.

Before you diminish or change your focus, you have to ask yourself, "If we can't make it here, what makes us believe we can make it somewhere else?" If you are truly expanding out of success, that is quite different, but if you are thinking that success will come to you easier on some other path, you are probably in for a rude awakening.

Every individual or corporation that experiences success does it with a singular focus, and then out of that success they build another success and one to follow that.

Every triumph comes with its own price and degree of sacrifice. If you take a detour trying to avoid the toll, you will quite often find the going gets even tougher and the toll still remains to be paid. For this reason, we should never get the "How are we going to do it?" mixed up in the "What are we going to do?" decision. This is always a mistake made by people who live lives of quiet desperation, as it has been so ably described.

You are going to pay the price, no matter what course you pursue, so you might as well pursue the course that creates excitement and passion for you. Then simply focus on your goal and the activities you know it will take to get you there. You will find that the shortest route to your ultimate destiny will take you directly through the most intimidating and daunting task that lies before you. But, as always, I am convinced that if you have a dream inside of you, it was put there because you have the capacity to perform every task necessary to reach that goal.

Today's the day!

R ecently, I heard about a group of advertising agencies that constantly seek what they call a "normal" city or town. Apparently, what they are looking for is the demographically perfect example of the United States. They spend a great deal of time searching for this elusive pocket of normality. Even when they find a city or town that they deem to be normal, within a year or two they have to move on because the existing site is—for whatever reason— no longer "normal."

As young children, we are all born as separate and distinct creative individuals. No matter what you may hear to the contrary, our society does not reward or appreciate unique individuals. We are taught at an early age to conform in every way so we will not stand out from the crowd. In essence, we are taught to be "normal."

This process of normalizing everyone is akin to seeking the lowest common human denominator. This is to say, if you never stand out you will certainly never be outstanding.

I will always remember being diagnosed with the disease that eventually resulted in my blindness. After it became apparent that I would slowly lose my sight and I would not be "normal," I remember my father saying, "Although you will never be normal, normal is really not anything worth aspiring to."

Although we would all agree with this in principle, as a society we still reward normality. While I would not advocate becoming antisocial, I do think greatness comes from individual creative expression. Think of all the things you do throughout your day. Ask yourself what would happen if you began performing a few of these tasks at a higher-than-normal level. Look at the mentors or people whose performance you aspire to. You will find that the real achievers in this world rarely do anything "normally." They perform a few critical tasks at the highest possible level and, quite often, ignore or delegate mundane tasks to others.

Monuments are never erected to normal people. They are erected to people dedicated to doing one thing exceedingly well. Find that thing in your life, and avoid the temptation to be normal.

Today's the day!

Your future, along with your personal and professional goals, is not as fragile as you might think. Failure is often the fertilizer that makes future success blossom. Recently, I had this principle confirmed to me by the story of nine Irishmen from the nineteenth century.

The story goes that in 1848, as Ireland was attempting to break away from England, nine young Irish rebels were captured and sentenced to death. As they were brought before Queen Victoria for punishment, she could not bear to have them executed, so she sent them to England's prison colony in Australia.

About forty years later, Queen Victoria visited Australia and was greeted by the prime minister, Sir Charles Gavan Duffy. She was shocked when he revealed that he had been one of those nine young Irishmen sentenced to die. Queen Victoria knighted him, and he became known as Lord Charles Duffy. The queen asked if Duffy had knowledge of the other eight prisoners. He informed her that they all had stayed in touch, and he told her of their accomplishments.

Thomas Francis Meagher immigrated to the United States, where he became a cattle baron and an early governor of Montana. Terrence McManus and Patrick Donahue both became generals in the United States Army, where they served with distinction. Richard O'Gorman immigrated to Canada, where he rose to become the governor general of Newfoundland. Morris Lyene and Michael Ireland both served as cabinet post members in Australia and served separately as Australia's attorney general. D'Arcy McGee became the prime minister of Canada. And, finally, John Mitchell immigrated to the United States, where he was a prominent New York politician. His son, also named John Mitchell, served as the mayor of New York City.

All of us face disappointments as well as obstacles and barriers on our different roads to success. I would not compare my problems with yours nor with those of our nine Irish friends. However, it is important to remember that we are only as big as the smallest thing it takes to divert us from our destiny.

Remember that in every defeat there lies a seed of a greater victory. Go out and find that seed, and you will live a marvelous life.

Today's the day!

Each time we interact with another person, we are given the opportunity to build either a bridge or a wall. There are no neutral meetings among people. Each contact either builds up or tears down the relationship.

Recently, I had the opportunity to have breakfast and lunch in the same hotel dining room on the same day. During breakfast, it was a bit crowded, and the food was somewhat slow in coming; however, the waitress was polite, pleasant, and professional. She inquired about me and the purpose of my trip. She seemed genuinely to care. I was left with a very positive impression of what otherwise could have been a mediocre to poor experience.

At noon that day, I returned for lunch. The dining room was nearly empty, and the food was prompt in arriving and fairly good; however, the waitress was not attentive and made me feel as though I was an intrusion in her otherwise important day. I was left with a negative impression even though all of the factors surrounding the meal were better than they had been in the morning with the exception of my communication with the waitress.

Millions of dollars are spent each day to advertise and lure customers to businesses. Great thought, effort, and preparation go into the details of the shopping or buying experience. Sometimes I think we forget that the customer will be left with a good or bad impression based on the human experience.

We need to view every interaction as a human bank account. Each time we are in contact with someone else, it is either a deposit or a withdrawal into their account. As you go about your day, try to be conscious of the fact that the strongest impression you leave about you or your business is probably your attitude and the way you communicate with others.

You have probably heard the phrase, "You never get a second chance to make a good first impression." While this is true, the reality goes much deeper. We never get another chance to redo any impression. They all count.

Today's the day!

F ear is the number one obstacle and barrier to all success. Often we are fooled into thinking that top performers are people who feel no fear. The reality is that champions feel the fear and perform in spite of it.

Shortly after losing my sight, I faced a fear that I had never before imagined. The only way to avoid everything that I was afraid of was to move into a little nine-by-twelve-foot room in the back of my house. This small room became my entire world.

Finally, one day in frustration I realized that everything I was afraid of outside of my room could not be any worse than spending the rest of my life in a nine-by-twelve-foot room. I decided to venture out as far as the mailbox at the end of my driveway.

The first time I stepped out of my house as a blind person and walked to my mailbox, I was barely moving and scared stiff. The five hundredth time I stepped out of my house and walked the length of my driveway, I didn't even think about being nervous. I just went to the mailbox and came back to the house.

I could just as easily have stumbled on the five-hundredth trip as I could have on the first, but by the time I'd made five hundred trips, I also knew that if I tripped over something, I could get up, dust myself off, and still get myself to the end of the driveway and back to the house.

Nothing about the driveway or the potential hazards had changed. *I* had changed. And that's the way it is with any success.

The problems and obstacles and challenges may not be any different. They may be bigger. But you and your ability to take on the challenge have grown even greater proportionally. You are better able to take the next step, and in that lies all the difference in the world.

Everyone feels the fear. Champions face the fear and live their destiny.

Today's the day!

Over twenty-five years ago, my father introduced me to a man who would become a mentor of mine and a very important influence in my life. Lee Braxton had an elementary-school education but made millions of dollars during the Depression and succeeded in many areas. He was one of those people who treated great people as if they were common, and he treated common people as if they were great. He improved the lives of many people around him. Mr. Braxton passed away many years ago, but I think of him almost daily.

Recently, my father was cleaning out some old files and ran across some items Mr. Braxton had written more than fifty years ago. Mr. Braxton's writings had to do with people who failed because they were afraid of success. At first glance, fear of success seems ridiculous. Everybody wants to be successful. Who would be afraid of it? The reality is that more people fail to achieve success because they have a deep-seated fear of it.

What we all seek is not necessarily success but our own comfort zone. We try to fit into the world in the way and at the levels we feel we deserve. You probably know people who are right on the verge of getting things they want and then, somehow, they almost sabotage their own efforts. Recently, I read about the phenomena of prisoners who, after serving their time, would commit some petty crime and go back to the penitentiary because that was where they felt most comfortable.

You have heard the old saying from people who disbelieve something: "I'll believe it when I see it." In reality, "You'll see it when you believe it." We are a product of what we believe and can imagine ourselves achieving. Anything beyond that takes us out of our comfort zone and creates the fear of success.

As you go through your day today, examine your long-term goals and objectives. Project yourself mentally into those roles that success will bring you. Determine whether that success role creates fear or comfort in your mind. You can often outperform what other people think of you, but you will never outperform what you think of yourself.

Today's the day!

PERSPECTIVE IS EVERYTHING

Reality can be best defined as one's perception based upon his or her perspective.

Recently, I was enjoying an old, rather antiquated spy novel in which four opposing secret agents are sitting around a table, engaged in a card game. One of the agents was to receive a coded symbol that he was to write on the tablecloth. The symbol would be picked up by a hidden camera in the ceiling of the room. The other three secret agents would observe the secret symbol as soon as it was written on the tablecloth and then report back to their respective spymasters.

At the appointed moment, one of the card players wrote the letter "M" on the tablecloth. The secret camera immediately picked up the symbol. The spy directly across the table abruptly excused himself and reported to his superiors that the symbol was a "W." At the same time, the two spies at the left and right sides of the table rushed to report that the secret symbol was a letter "E" and the number "3," respectively.

While the novel was otherwise forgettable, it was interesting to note that four trained observers—each with a goal as simple as identifying one character—all arrived at a different conclusion. The spies failed in their mission, not because they weren't observant or thorough, but because they didn't understand the rule of perspective.

You've heard it said that beauty is in the eye of the beholder. Everything is in the eye or the perception of the beholder. In order to work with people, you must be willing to understand, consider, and appreciate their perspective.

We have all met people who have a positive, upbeat outlook on life. From their perspective, they've just eaten the greatest meal, seen the most beautiful sunset in history, or heard the most wonderful music. On the other hand, we all know people who take a more cautious approach to describing life. From their perspective, the meal was OK, the sunset was somewhat enjoyable, and the music sounded all right.

In reality, these two individuals are describing the exact same things, and unless you understand and calibrate people's perspectives, you will be misled and fail to get the information and feedback you need in order to succeed. When we understand people's perspectives, we begin to truly communicate feelings instead of words.

Today's the day!

W hat is it that causes some people to perform at an extremely high level while other people seem to be mired in mediocrity? This is a question that has plagued those who have studied personal development since the beginning of time. There may be an answer hiding in an unlikely spot.

Those who have overcome obstacles in their own life seem to be better prepared to face the world's challenges.

Recently, I read Tom Brokaw's book *The Greatest Generation.* In this book, he explains why he believes the generation that came of age during World War II was the greatest of the twentieth century. Brokaw makes an extremely good case for this. However, when you delve into the cause for this generation's greatness, it can be a bit baffling.

Initially, one would think that their greatness came from the extra training they received to go into World War II or maybe the additional education they received as a result of the GI Bill after the war. In reality, their greatness was formed much earlier. As a result of living through the Great Depression and then struggling through World War II, they came face-to-face with their own potential.

You have heard it said that any adversity that does not destroy you makes you stronger. This principle accounts for the greatest generation in Brokaw's book. Once you have faced adversity and stared it down, you have the ability to calmly deal with other barriers, while those who have never faced adversity question their own ability.

If you look throughout the pages of history at those who have accomplished the feats that we all aspire to, you will find that the seeds of their greatness were planted in their own adversity. Their seeds were fertilized with failure and watered with the blood, sweat, and tears of personal struggle. The next time you face adversity, disappointment, or discouragement, realize that herein lies the seed of a greater tomorrow.

The struggle you face today is the springboard to your destiny.

Today's the day!

FIND THE RIGHT GAME

We've all been taught that there are two kinds of people in the world—the winners and the losers. But, like any other belief that we all hold dear, it's not quite that simple. The reality is that everyone potentially is a winner. They are simply competing in the wrong game.

The skill level and passion needed to become a champion will not transfer from game to game. When the sports history of the twentieth century was written, sports writers debated as to who should be considered the century's greatest athlete. Virtually all agreed that if he was not the best, Michael Jordan was certainly among the top two or three athletes of the past 100 years.

But even the great Michael Jordan, who rewrote the record books in basketball, was nothing more than a mediocre minor league baseball player.

If you're not currently a champion in your life, it may be because you're in the wrong game. Your talents, skills, ability, and passion are perfectly suited for you to become a winner. If you're not winning, instead of trying harder, you may want to get in another competition.

There comes a time when we all have to be brutally honest about our own strengths and weaknesses. As a blind person I realize that there are many things I simply do not have the capacity to accomplish in the traditional manner. However, any "disability" can become an advantage in that it limits the games you will not win at, so the games where you can become a champion become obvious.

Find the thing you enjoy, and you will find yourself putting in the effort and the intensity necessary to become a champion. As long as you're playing someone else's game according to their rules, you will be frustrated. But once you take that bold step out of the darkness into the sunshine and begin to pursue your own passion, you will find yourself with the gold medal of life hanging around your neck as you stand on that top step.

Victory is sweet, and it belongs to each of us. In final analysis the reward comes as much from doing the right thing as it does from performing well.

Today's the day!

I have long been a fan of golf tournaments presented on television. Recently, Tiger Woods has revolutionized the sport and has altered the way the audience enjoys an event.

In a recent tournament, Tiger was putting on the last hole in order to win the four-day tournament. The dignified professional announcer intoned, "This is the one shot that will win the whole tournament."

As Tiger Woods did, indeed, make the putt and win the tournament, I thought about the fact that any of the 275 shots over the four-day period could have won or lost the championship. The first shot was no less important than the last. It didn't hold the immediate and certain promise of victory, but it was, nevertheless, just as significant.

Our lives and careers work the same way. We go through our days performing many seemingly insignificant activities that, when combined, make up our success or failure. Every time you meet someone, draft a letter, make a presentation, answer a phone call, or any one of a hundred other things, you are performing an activity that could conceivably in and of itself make you a winner or a loser.

Unlike Tiger Woods, you and I never know which activity is going to make the difference. That moment when you were less than your best could have far-reaching consequences. You never know who's watching your performance.

If we knew which were the critical turning points in our lives, we would perform as if in the Olympics, the World Series, or the Super Bowl, but we never know. Therefore, in order to be a winner, we have to perform every shot to a standard of excellence. As a good friend of mine says, "A winner is a winner all the time."

Champions don't get a day off.

Today's the day!

WHY AND WHY NOT?

I am reminded of a quote that became famous at Robert Kennedy's memorial service. "Some men see things as they are and say 'Why?' I dream of things that never were and say, 'Why not?'"

In our society, we have become so risk-averse that we often endanger creativity. We hire consultants to tell us what is possible, but they define "possible" by determining what has already been done. It is important to realize that prior to every great advancement of humankind, the experts of the day would have assured you that it was impossible.

Often when I speak to audiences, I ask them to go into a state of mind I call "neutral." This simply means to suspend the circumstances surrounding their immediate reality and examine the world of possibility. This is not as easy to do as it would seem. We have been programmed to avoid risk and measure every obstacle. So, as soon as you begin exploring possibilities by asking yourself "Why wouldn't this be possible?" your mind immediately begins counting the cost, the risk, and the probability of failure.

Please understand that we need people who examine the risk and deal with the details. They are the people who propel the ship of human endeavor. However, the captain of the ship—the person who controls the helm and the rudder—should be a big-picture "Why not?" sort of person.

Everything was impossible before it was done. For decades prior to Roger Bannister breaking the four-minute-mile, it was assumed that that mark was unattainable. Within several years of Bannister's record-breaking run, literally dozens of athletes around the world broke the four-minute-mile.

Visionaries open the door of possibility allowing the whole world to pass into a better, brighter, and more significant existence.

Whether you agree with Robert Kennedy's politics is unimportant. The lasting legacy I hope he leaves us is that of always questioning reality and expanding the realm of possibility.

Look at every area of your life and ask the question "Why?" Then go into neutral long enough to explore all of the possibilities and ask yourself, "Why not?" You may begin to live your life at a higher level, fueled by the power of possibility.

Today's the day!

S uccess and happiness in life come when we begin to understand that the universal rules apply to us.

Remember when you were a teenager? You were never going to get old. The concept of being thirty was so foreign to you that it did not have meaning. Then, before you know it, you are thirty, but you are certain that you'll never be as old as forty. I can remember being a small child and unaware that the law of gravity did, indeed, apply to me. A few bumps and bruises later, the reality became clear.

Recently, the correction in the stock market taught a lot of naive investors that the rules apply to them. For several years, the market was so strong that many new investors had never seen a down market. If you had asked them, they would have assured you that, in theory, the market can go down. But by the way they borrowed and invested on margin, their actions indicated they weren't convinced the rules applied to them.

Many people have difficulty seeing rules with long-term consequences in a daily perspective. They are aware that wearing a seatbelt is important to their safety, but they say things like, "I'm just going to the store or down the block." Although they know in a lifetime perspective, it is critical, it never occurs to them that the rules apply to them today. It's never *this* cigarette, or *this* drink, or *that* bad habit today that is going to create the problem.

When we fail in life, it's rarely because we don't know what to do. More often, we fail because we don't do what we know. Success becomes a habit, and failure can be habit-forming as well. We have all heard people who have just experienced failure say, "I knew that was going to happen," or "That always happens to me." At the same time, those who succeed follow the rules of success, and their victories follow one another like clockwork.

Customer service means treating everyone by the Golden Rule—

treating them in your place of business as you would like to be treated in theirs. We never know which prospect will turn into the multimillion-dollar relationship. Therefore, you have to treat everyone with a high degree of integrity and professionalism. If we knew when we were going to have the wreck, we would all wear the seatbelt only on that day. Because we don't, we apply universal rules of success to all situations. In this way, we can make every day a safe, productive, and successful experience.

Today's the day!

In the past few years, I have had the privilege of writing several books and a number of syndicated columns. Several years ago, I completed my first novel, which has since been made into a major motion picture. Writing fiction is a venture into a new arena, as you have the privilege of writing about the world and the way you think it should be instead of the way it really is.

Without spoiling the story, when one of the richest men in the country dies, he leaves all of his relatives money, businesses, or property, with the exception of one young man. He leaves his grandson a twelve-month odyssey that results in *The Ultimate Gift*.

Life is a gift that has been given to us. The way we live it and maximize it is our gift to those around us. Following is a list of just a few of life's gifts that we all can enjoy as outlined in *The Ultimate Gift*:

1. *The Gift of Work:* He who loves his work never labors.
2. *The Gift of Money:* Money is nothing more than a tool. It can be a force for good, a force for evil, or simply be idle.
3. *The Gift of Friends:* It is a wealthy person, indeed, who calculates riches not in gold but in friends.
4. *The Gift of Learning:* Education is a lifelong journey whose destination expands as you travel.
5. *The Gift of Problems:* Problems may only be avoided by exercising good judgment. Good judgment may only be gained by experiencing life's problems.
6. *The Gift of Family:* Some people are born into wonderful families. Others have to find or create them. Being a member of a family is a priceless membership that we pay nothing for but love.
7. *The Gift of Laughter:* Laughter is good medicine for the soul. Our world is desperately in need of more medicine.

8. *The Gift of Dreams:* Faith is all that dreamers need to see into the future.

9. *The Gift of Giving:* The only way you can truly get more out of life for yourself is to give part of yourself away.

10. *The Gift of Gratitude*: In those times we yearn to have more in our lives, we should dwell on the things we already have. In doing so, we will often find that our lives are already full to overflowing

11. *The Gift of a Day:* Life at its essence boils down to one day at a time. Today's the day!

12. *The Gift of Love:* Love is a treasure for which we can never pay. The only way we keep it is to give it away.

13. *The Ultimate Gift:* In the end, life lived to its fullest is its own *Ultimate Gift.*

Begin to live your life today as an expression of *The Ultimate Gift.*

Today's the day!

Thinking Inside and Outside of the Box

T he current buzz phrase among business and creative types is, "Thinking outside of the box." This means that you think in nonorthodox, nontraditional ways that lead you to new and creative conclusions. This is a powerful tool, as far as it goes, because it allows you to use your entire creative mind without limiting yourself to the way things have always been done. However, while you're thinking in the new "out of the box" way, don't forget that there are some pretty great concepts in that old box. Traditional thinking at one time was someone's creative "out of the box" thinking. Because it was successful, that thought became traditional or "in the box."

Recently, I heard about a woman who was interested in bringing her kitchen into the computer age. She bought a computer program for storing all of her recipes. Then she took her old laminated recipe cards out of her old wooden recipe box. She went to the computer in her home office and spent many hours entering all of her recipes into her personal computer. After completing the monumental task, she was ready to start cooking with her new twenty-first-century recipe system.

She selected a dish she wanted to prepare, and her computer instantly retrieved the recipe and displayed it on the screen. She went into the kitchen and began cooking. Very quickly she realized that she was wasting all of her time running back and forth between the kitchen and her computer down the hall in her home office. Her solution to this problem was to print the recipe on a piece of computer paper so she could bring the recipe into the kitchen. Before long, as often happens in an active kitchen, the countertop became a mess and the computer printout containing her recipe became soaked, stained, and illegible.

In utter frustration, she said, "It would be great if I had all of my recipes printed out on waterproof, stain-proof cards." If you're following the progression, you will realize her new wish looks an awful lot like where she started—with laminated recipe cards in a wooden box.

Don't think about whether it's a new idea or an old idea. Don't worry about whether it is in the box or out of it. Remove the box and implement the best idea.

Today's the day!

As you have more milestone birthdays—the ones that end in "0"—you come to learn the myriad of things you don't know. Life's experiences give us wisdom, but for every answer there seems to be two questions that pop up that are not answered.

When you were a teenager or a young adult, everything seemed simple, easy, and you fully understood it all. As time passed, the simple black-and-white world faded into several complex shades of gray. We come to realize that people are products of their environment, their thinking, and their attitudes.

Often it seems that ignorant and uninitiated people want to tell you everything, while wise and learned people seem reluctant to speak. I believe that it is almost a universal law that people's opinions that are forced on you are generally worthless, while those individuals who really have something to say must be sought out and questioned. Don't ever ask anyone's opinion who doesn't have what you want. On the other hand, when you find people who have succeeded in the arena of your interest, you must specifically ask them for their wisdom.

As younger people, we think there is only one side to an issue. As we get older, we discover there are two sides, and when wisdom is really gained, we learn there are many sides with varying angles. Time, experience, books, and travel all expand one's field of reference. Meeting different people from different places either in person or through books will cause us to think. Small-minded people often only associate with or read material from people with whom they agree. Wise people will discuss issues or read books written by people with whom they may not agree.

Wisdom is achieved by keeping an open mind and a closed

mouth. On the other hand, ignorance is exposed by having an open mouth and a closed mind. Commit yourself to listen more than you talk, and be sure that you are listening to people who have something worth saying. Each day, you make either a deposit or a withdrawal in your life's bank account of wisdom. Be sure to invest and save wisely.

Today's the day!

The Commitment Continuum

We've all heard the story of the person asked to walk the length of a two-by-four board while it's lying on the ground. Obviously, it's no problem. Then this person is asked to walk the length of the same board for $1 million—the only difference being that the board will be stretched between two skyscrapers, 1,000 feet off the ground. Here, there are very few takers, because most of us would not risk our lives—even for $1 million—to balance on a four-inch-wide board a thousand feet in the air.

However, if we were to add one more detail and say that your child's life is at stake, and your child is on the other building, and the only way to get there is across the two-by-four, the scenario becomes simple. The only thing that changes from the board on the ground to the board in the air is the amount of risk and commitment it takes to proceed.

You have probably been told at some point that you must have total commitment toward everything you do in your life. Not only is this not true, it is dangerous. There are only a few things in life where you can invest your total commitment, so we must choose our commitments wisely. You should obviously have total commitment to your spouse and your family. You should have total commitment to your faith or the core beliefs that you live by. And you should have total commitment toward your destiny or the life's passion you have chosen. But if you have the same level of commitment to your favorite TV program that you have toward your family, you have a serious problem in your life.

Balance in life means having the right amount of commitment invested in the appropriate things for you. Make sure that all commitments really belong to you and are not ones that you have been forced into or feel pressured into from other people.

I have heard it said that if there is nothing worth dying for, there is very little worth living for. This is a dramatic way of saying, "Make sure that all your commitments are in the right places for you." Each day, be certain that as you invest your time, effort, and energy, they line up with the commitments you hold most dear in your life.

Today's the day!

THE FATHER OF INVENTION

If necessity is the mother of invention, desperation must certainly be its father. Many people labor under the false impression that creativity and innovation come from having time in a carefree environment to reflect on possibilities and think "out of the box." In reality, so much of what we call new developments or innovations came from a desperate need brought to the forefront by a pressing problem.

Recently, I was reminded of the story of the ice-cream vendor at the World's Fair a century ago who found himself in the unenviable position of having virtually a limitless supply of customers while running out of spoons and bowls for his ice cream. His ice-cream stand was situated next to a waffle vendor who was unsympathetically criticizing the ice-cream vendor for being ill prepared.

At a moment of frustration and desperation, the flash of genius came. The ice-cream vendor went next door to the waffle stand, bought hundreds of waffles, and formed them into what we all know today to be ice-cream cones.

The ice-cream cone made the gentleman at the ice-cream stand at the World's Fair a millionaire many times over, but what really inspired his genius was not the level of necessity but the interjection of a degree of desperation. It's amazing what we can do when we have to perform.

So many businesses today are run in a bureaucratic fashion. A certain amount of this organizational style is critical, but what is lost is the entrepreneurial creativity. An entrepreneur stays alive by making something happen. A bureaucrat stays alive by avoiding making an obvious mistake. Therefore, the entrepreneur is propelled to do something, even if it may not instantly be the perfect course. The bureaucrat, on the other hand, becomes stagnant and often chooses to surround himself with a defense made up of reports and studies showing that the best course of action is to do nothing.

As you run your life or your business, try to find the balance between the orderly control of the bureaucrat—which will allow you to keep the day-to-day system running—and the creativity of the entrepreneur. The next time you are enjoying an ice-cream cone, remember that it came more from a last-minute attempt to overcome a devastating mistake than any creative genius. Today, vow to look for opportunity disguised as crisis.

Today's the day!

Ẇe hear a lot these days about the various theories of financial planning. As the stock market provides its ongoing roller-coaster ride, there seems to be a proliferation of "financial experts" lining up to tell you what to do with your money.

Financial planning is vital but not necessarily the kind that the "experts" want you to buy into. How you utilize your money and the financial priorities you set will have a great deal to do with the way you live your life. It's a lot like ordering dinner in a restaurant. There are no right or wrong answers, but if you take the advice of an "expert," you may end up eating liver when you really wanted seafood.

When you really analyze it, there are only three things your money will buy. You can spend your money on things, memories, or security. Once again, among the three choices, there are no right or wrong answers. As in most cases, a degree of balance and personal preference is the key to happiness.

We have all seen people who go overboard buying things. They have to have the newest car and the latest fashions. While there is nothing innately wrong in having things, if it is your only pursuit, you will never be totally satisfied. The advertisers on Madison Avenue in New York City are working overtime to make sure that there is always something new you have to have in order to feel good about yourself— if you are one of those people dominated by the things that you have or, more appropriately, by the things that have you.

There are those who spend their money on creating wonderful experiences that translate into memories that can never be taken away from them. This is a wonderful pursuit if kept in balance. But if you go overboard in creating memories and experiences, you become a card-carrying member of the "eat, drink, and be merry, for tomorrow we die" club. Many people have found that experiences and memories are not enough to sustain them through retirement or a financial crisis.

Security is an important goal, but you can't invest all your money for a "rainy day." If you're not careful, you can miss the wonderful experience of today and then find out that it may not rain tomorrow. Find the balance between things, memories, and security, and you will be your own financial expert.

Today's the day!

The word "entrepreneur" has come to mean a person who is in business for him or herself. While I cannot disagree with this definition, aren't we all in business for ourselves? Even the most entrenched middle manager in the midst of a huge corporate bureaucracy is really in his own business. Several years ago, the term "intrapreneur" was developed to mean those people or groups who had some autonomy within a corporate structure. As we broaden that definition, we must come to realize that all of us are in business for ourselves.

There is a big push in corporate America to have a corporate mission statement or a corporate goal. When you take all the people away, there is no corporation. Therefore, a corporation cannot have a goal or a mission statement. Instead, the mission statement would be a compilation of all of the individual hopes, dreams, and aspirations of the people who work there.

A good corporate goal would be a goal that will be reached when each of the individuals within a corporation collectively reach their own goals, therefore achieving the corporate objective. Too often in corporate America, people who have no choice in the matter are asked to buy into corporate goals. While these demands will get you lip service, they won't result in the passion that is required to achieve excellence.

It is important to find out what will motivate the people you work with. It's not always money, titles, big offices, or a reserved parking space. While these things have their place, more often, people are motivated by being appreciated, feeling valuable, and having a sense of accomplishment within the grand scheme of things.

Many corporations have a policy that each employee should come in for a monthly or quarterly review of his or her performance. Instead of having an executive arbitrarily review an employee's performance, I would prefer to see that executive ask the employee, "What are your goals over the next month, and how can we help you get there?"

Only when we realize that we're all in the same boat do we understand the importance of having everyone pulling in the same direction. It's not critical that everyone within a corporation understand the same big picture. The next time you get on an airplane, look around at all the other passengers and realize that over the next few hours, you may all be going to the same place, but you don't have the same objectives in mind. Some people are going on a business trip while others are going home. Some of your fellow passengers will be connecting to other planes while still others will have a long drive at the end of their flight. There are as many reasons for traveling as there are people on the airplane, but—in the short term—they all agree on their destination and are pulling in the same direction.

See yourself and the people you work with as individual entrepreneurs with their own goals, talents, and passions. When you find these inner secrets of the people around you, you will also find the key to individual and corporate success.

Today's the day!

M ost of us take a day out of our busy schedules to observe Labor Day. For the majority of people across the country, Labor Day represents the last long weekend of summer. It's a time to take one more trip to the beach, the lake, or our favorite camping spot. Labor Day also creates a good opportunity for us to take a quick look at this thing we call "work."

Other than our name, there is nothing that defines us more in our society than our work. When we meet a stranger, after the obligatory exchange of names, the most comfortable question and topic of conversation is work. "What do you do?" Not only do others define us by our work, but also we, indeed, define ourselves.

The late, great George Burns once said, "If you love your job, you'll never work a day in your life." The reason Mr. Burns lived and worked the better part of a full century was because it was obvious he loved his work. When you think about our hectic pace and packed schedules, it is quite likely that you spend much more time with the people you work with than you spend with your family. If we are going to define ourselves by our work, have those around us identify us by our profession, and spend more time working than we do with the people we love, isn't it critical that we choose the right career path?

If you do not find power, passion, and fulfillment in your daily work, it is time for you to start making plans for a change. Most of us, if we are truly honest, selected our career based on money considerations. This is a huge mistake. While I recognize the imperative nature of paying the bills, the top performers in every field of endeavor are very well compensated.

Don't get so busy making a living that you forget to create a life.

Today's the day!

You've heard it said that two heads are better than one. This would, of course, depend upon which two heads we're talking about, but—all things being equal—there is strength and wisdom in numbers. The farther up the mountain of success you travel, the less populated you will find your path to be. Achievement and excellence bring a degree of isolation.

No one should ever make a decision in a vacuum. As you progress closer and closer to your goals, however, it becomes more difficult to find people whose advice and counsel are appropriate.

One of the keys to seeking counsel is to never ask someone's advice if they don't already have what you are trying to obtain as you pursue your goals. It is not critical that they be on the same path, but it is vital that they share the critical elements of your success.

In an interview, Tiger Woods revealed that he, Charles Barkley, and Michael Jordan speak either in person or on the telephone a minimum of once a week. They have found that they share life challenges relating to athletic performance, financial success, and living in the public eye. The fact that Tiger Woods is a golfer and Michael Jordan a basketball player is really not important relating to these areas of mutual interest.

Whether these high-performing athletes realize it, they have formed a mastermind group. A mastermind group is nothing more or less than a group of like-minded individuals who are dealing with the same obstacles and challenges. Recently, I formed such a group with four other colleagues from the speaking profession. We all speak on slightly different topics and move in varied circles; however, when it comes to the basic day-to-day challenges surrounding the growth and success of our businesses, we are each in the same game. We set our own rules, and we each establish our own goals. We depend on one another for honest feedback and accountability.

I would encourage you to find several like-minded individuals who are traveling on the same road or at least a similar road toward success, and form your own mastermind group. The dividends you will both give and receive can be immeasurable.

Today's the day!

BE PREPARED

Here in Tulsa, Oklahoma, we have just experienced one of our brief annual snow and ice storms. They come often enough to remind us that it is still winter, but they come seldom enough that we can't adequately prepare.

Each year after our perfunctory winter storm, the same old arguments resurface. "Why don't we have adequate snowplows and other equipment to take care of this situation?" I'm not saying we couldn't be better prepared; however, the obvious answer is that we cannot justify the commitment and expense it would take to prepare for something that happens so infrequently.

The same "be prepared" arguments arise when we look at business and personal finances. There are people who spend all of their resources preparing for a rainy day, and then there are people who go to the other extreme. They believe they should "eat, drink, and be merry, for tomorrow we die." This live-now versus security argument is one that we face every day—not just when it snows.

Money is a tool and, thus, can only buy us things, memories, or security. Those who invest too heavily in security soon learn that we all have to live, and the only thing that security offers us is the opportunity to live and experience life in the future. If security only enables you to exchange today's experiences for those you might enjoy in the future, it is a bad trade-off.

On the other hand, if you spend all of your resources experiencing today without a thought to the future, you are like the farmer who eats his seed corn. You can have a banquet immediately, but you will be starving when the harvest rolls around.

As someone who began my business career as an investment broker, I realize that in many of these decisions, there is no right or wrong answer. It is dependent upon the temperament of each organization or individual. We must all ask ourselves: What is our true risk tolerance, and how can we survive the worst-case scenario? While every risk cannot be avoided, we must manage those risks that are most likely to come our way.

Look in the mirror and seek the honest answers within yourself, and then you will find the balance between living today and enjoying tomorrow.

Today's the day!

Whether it is in your personal or professional life, The Golden Rule still applies: Do unto others as you would have them do unto you. Too often in business, we spend all of our time on one side of the equation and fail to see things from the perspective of our customers. Systems, policies, and procedures that make total sense to you because you deal with them daily may be a complete and utter mystery to your customers.

Recently, I had the occasion to make a major equipment purchase for my business. After being shuffled from one department to the next, told to "Wait," to "Come back later," and "There's no one here that can help you," I realized that in a free-enterprise, market-driven economy, I was working way too hard to spend my money. Customer service is the key to any successful business that deals with the public or even in a business-to-business environment.

Whenever possible, call your business on the main number simply to experience how the phone is answered. You may be in for a surprise. A national survey indicated that six out of ten businesses could not be identified by the average caller, even though the operator supposedly answered the phone with the name of the business. In addition to being polite and professional, phone people must speak distinctly so that their name and the name of the organization can be clearly understood.

Seek feedback from clients or customers who walk into your place of business or conduct their transactions online or via the mail. It doesn't matter how convenient it is for you. It matters greatly how convenient it is for your customer.

Whenever possible, empower the people who deal with customer complaints and problems to resolve the problem immediately. Customers with complaints reported a satisfactory resolution to their problems in direct proportion to how few people they were forced to speak with and how little paperwork they were required to complete. Proper customer service can turn a complaint into a long-term positive relationship and can turn your current customers and clients into an ongoing sales and marketing tool for your business.

That old wisdom still applies: Your customers do not care how much you know until they know how much you care. Today, resolve to let your customers know how valuable they truly are.

Today's the day!

Spring is the season of the year when many of us take it upon ourselves to clean out closets, attics, and garages. I must admit that this time of year brings renewed hope and energy to me, but it has never presented me with an overwhelming desire to clean. However, as we explore the new life all around us, it can be a good time to do some very important spring-cleaning as it relates to our lives.

Think of the old habits that we do for no reason other than we have always done them, and explore which of these are keeping us from where we want to be. Many of our habits need a thorough spring-cleaning. Spring is a great time of year to examine our habits and the way we invest our time, effort, and energy and determine whether these patterns are worth keeping.

Anything in your closet that you have not worn in a year can probably safely be discarded. Any habit that you have not thought about in a similar length of time needs to be dragged out into the light of day and really explored for its value or lack thereof.

Just as two things cannot occupy the same space, and the universe will not allow a void to exist, a bad or nonproductive habit needs to be replaced with a good habit. Psychologists tell us that anything we do for twenty-one days will begin to become a habit. This is to say that on the twenty-second day, if you do not perform the ritual activity it will seem as if something is missing.

If we are, indeed, creatures of habit—which we are—it is incumbent upon us to form good habits. All creatures in the animal kingdom have habits. They are called instincts. We have the privilege, unique among all creatures, of determining what our habits will be.

You are one quality decision away from anything you want,

because you change your life when you change your mind. When you change your mind, you will change your habits, and changing your habits will inevitably change your life.

Today's the day!

FOUR HURDLES TO STARTING A BUSINESS

When it comes to career, one of the greatest dreams of many people is to own their own business. This dream paints a mental picture of being the captain of one's own ship and being in control of one's destiny. Most people who are considered a world-class success in business own or at least run their own operation. For the right person, there is nothing better than owning your own business. For the wrong person, there is nothing worse than owning your own business. For the right people, starting or running a company becomes liberating, creatively stimulating, and energizing. For the wrong people, it becomes pressure-filled, confining, and paralyzing.

There are a number of hurdles that you should consider before starting or running your own business. These hurdles build upon one another. You don't go to the second hurdle until you have successfully cleared the first one, and unless you get over all the hurdles, you should not even consider being in business for yourself. Once you're over the last hurdle, it doesn't mean you win the race. It means you qualify to enter the starting blocks to begin the competition of owning and running your own business.

Always remember, there is nothing wrong with not being a business owner, leader, or entrepreneur. There are scores of people who function valuably and professionally within someone else's corporate structure. This does not make them bad people. On the contrary, it makes them very good people at fitting into a vibrant team.

The following hurdles should each be successfully cleared before you move on toward the possibility of even considering starting or running your own business.

Hurdle 1: Honestly assess your temperament to determine whether you are suited to be an entrepreneur or business owner. Are you a leader? Do you enjoy blazing your own trail, or would you prefer to follow someone else's lead or a clearly delineated job description and career path? Ask friends, coworkers, and family members who will be honest with you to assess your temperament as well. Often, those around us see our strengths and weaknesses more clearly than we can.

Hurdle 2: Determine whether you have a unique talent, ability, or opportunity. You have heard that if you build a better mousetrap, people will beat a path to your door. Obviously, it would be best to be the very first person to create a mousetrap. If not, you must determine if your mousetrap is really better and has either a cost- or a quality-competitive advantage compared to those currently on the market. You must also assess whether there are a sufficient number of mice—or in this case, potential customers—in your proposed marketplace. This area cannot be overemphasized. Entrepreneurs fail every day because they are not honest with themselves. They feel they have a unique talent, product, or marketplace that no one else has.

Hurdle 3: Do you have enough capital? Most entrepreneurs will tell you the term "enough capital" does not exist. There is more truth than one might imagine in that statement. When you are in business for yourself, everything takes longer, costs more, and is more difficult than you imagined. This is not negative thinking. It is the real-life experience of most business owners. Too many would-be entrepreneurs base all projections on the proverbial best-case scenario. You would be much better off to base your projections on the worst-case scenario and even cut it in half. If you can survive in that environment, you have an excellent chance of making it. The only cardinal sin in business planning is to run out of money. Money buys you time, second chances, and many lessons. With money, you're like a pilot flying 40,000 feet above the earth. Any problems can be dealt with at this altitude. You have a lot of time to make corrections and contingency plans and to pursue alternatives. Without enough capital, you are like that same pilot flying 100 feet above the ground. You can fly successfully if everything goes perfectly; but if there's one mechanical error, fuel problem, or wind sheer, you are destined to crash and burn.

Hurdle 4: Do you have a passion for your new business? This may be the most critical hurdle of all. It has to be more than a good idea or an attractive business. You have to be willing to live, eat, and breathe your new venture because, in reality, you will probably be forced to. Becoming an entrepreneur means that you are willing to do things that most people are not willing to do. This is only possible when you have an unbelievable passion to pursue your dream of owning your own business.

If you have gotten over these four hurdles, you may be ready to approach the starting line. If you are, indeed, going to launch into your own business, above all remember the best advice I ever heard about being in business for myself: Make sure you're having fun. You got into this because you thought you would enjoy it. If you don't enjoy being in business for yourself, you would be far better off having a job working for someone else.

On your mark. Get set. Go!

Today's the day!

W e have all had a brief memory lapse during which we forgot someone's name, a phone number, or simply what we came into a room to get. While these things can be annoying, they are usually not critical to our overall success and happiness. On the other hand, what is critical to our overall success and happiness is to reduce the important elements of life to writing.

Most people would not consider going to the grocery store without a written list of things they want to purchase. But these same people might laugh if you asked them to write down their life goals, objectives, or creative ideas. These are powerful thoughts and merit the effort necessary to write them down so that you can refer to them in the future.

Many of us have had the frustrating experience of having a great thought or idea in the middle of the night and then drifting off to sleep, convinced that when we implement our new idea in the morning, everything will be wonderful. The next morning, however, while we remember that we had a great idea or thought, we just can't remember what it was. It would be impossible to measure the untold number of ideas, creative thoughts, and wonderful breakthroughs that will never see the light of day because someone failed to take them seriously enough to write down.

I have been writing these columns, weekly, for several years. When I completed my first column, I was convinced it contained all of the wisdom and knowledge that I possessed. Then after the second and third weeks, I was convinced that I was running out of material. But, at some point, I got into the habit of writing down as many ideas as possible when they occurred to me. Sometimes, in meetings in the office or during various conversations, one of my staff members will exclaim excitedly, "That's a column!" And I recognize a seed of a great idea that I was about to overlook.

Get in the habit of recognizing and identifying great ideas, thoughts, and goals. Then be sure to write them down. If it's good enough for your shopping list, it's good enough for your life.

Today's the day!

I n business and in life, one of the keys to success is avoiding bad situations. Unfortunately, bad situations rarely come with a label that identifies them as such. Experience and maturity bring us the ability to identify bad situations earlier or, hopefully, before they occur, but we are always faced with the challenge.

Several years ago, I came across a meaningful decision-making principle that I call "accelerate the point of failure." The essence of this principle is that when it comes to bad situations, it is best to identify them before you get involved; however, if you are already involved, it is vital to identify the bad situation and eliminate it as quickly as possible. The only thing worse than failing today in an endeavor is to work hard for a year and then realize the endeavor was doomed to fail from the beginning. If a weak link or critical element is hanging in the balance, it is best to expose the weakness and deal with it immediately as opposed to waiting.

Let's assume you are building a house, and the only thing that makes the project financially feasible for you is to use some new water-resistant roofing material that was introduced to you by a questionable salesperson. It sounds too good to be true because it is very inexpensive, but the salesperson assures you it is water-resistant. Ordinarily, this roofing material would be the last thing applied to your new house; however, the principle of "accelerating your point of failure" tells us that the thing to do instead of waiting until the last minute to determine whether the roofing material performs as promised is to test it now to see whether it works. If it does function as promised, you can go ahead and build your house with confidence; however, if it doesn't work as promised, you will not even dig the foundation—much less complete 99 percent of the work—before determining that your project was doomed to fail. By moving the weak link in the chain to the starting line instead of the finish line, you can save an immense amount of time, effort, energy, and resources.

Avoid bad situations when you can, but when you can't, expose them and eliminate them as quickly as possible.

Today's the day!

S uccess in business or personal life is a result of overcoming problems. The only thing necessary to have a great idea is to go about your daily activities and wait for a problem to arise. Ask yourself, "How can I avoid or overcome this problem?" Your answer is a great idea. The only thing you need to do to have a great business opportunity is to ask yourself, "How can I help other people avoid or overcome that same problem?" Your answer will be an opportunity.

Solving problems requires a different perspective. Albert Einstein said, "It is impossible to solve a problem with the same mind that created the problem." When you observe a set of circumstances and perceive it to be a problem, remember that your mind is what created the problem. The same set of circumstances viewed by another person might not be perceived as a problem. It may appear to them to be an opportunity or a brief detour along the road to success.

For all the people who identify problems and simply stop all progress toward their goals, I can show you more people with the same set of circumstances who have used their problems as springboards to even greater success and opportunity. Often, problems are like a movie set in a horror film. They appear very scary and menacing at first glance. But if you walk around to the other side and gain another perspective, you discover that it is nothing more than canvas and cardboard being held up by a few random two-by-fours.

Don't be afraid to embrace a problem and look at it from all sides. Seek the opinions of others that you respect, but don't pollute their thinking by identifying the circumstances as a problem. Simply lay out the facts and get their perspective on the situation. Problems and opportunities rarely come labeled as such.

Look for the benefit. Seek the hidden treasure. You will always find what you are looking for. If you go through the day today looking for problems, you will find them. If, instead, you look for solutions and opportunities, they will appear everywhere. Determine to look for the key to your success in every situation.

Today's the day!

THE MYTH OF FAIRNESS

Fairness is an ever-elusive concept. It is something we should always strive for while realizing that it can never be achieved. Much of the animosity, anxiety, and stress that people experience today is due to their assumption of fairness. Let us once and for all dispel the age-old myth. Life is not fair.

This does not mean we should accept inequities as a part of our ongoing lives, but it does mean that we live in an imperfect world, and we are all subject to its whims.

I recently had a conversation with a friend of mine who is a prominent attorney. He just returned from a working trip to California. During his stay, he made a reservation at an outstanding restaurant on the ocean for dinner one evening. While he was making the reservation, he specifically requested a table outside and asked the maître d' if he would be allowed to smoke a cigar outside after dinner. The maître d' assured him that he would confirm his reservation for a table outdoors and that he could, indeed, smoke his cigar after dinner.

On the appointed evening, my friend had a wonderful dinner and, afterward, took out one of his prized cigars and lit it, prepared to enjoy sunset over the Pacific Ocean. Immediately, his waiter rushed over and informed him that he would not be allowed to smoke his cigar as it was against the restaurant policy and, furthermore, against Californian law. My friend explained that he had already spoken with the maître d' and had been assured that everything was OK. Nevertheless, the waiter insisted that he put out his cigar and left him sitting alone with his extinguished cigar as the sun slowly sank into the ocean.

My friend was faced, at that very moment, with the dilemma that we all have to deal with from time to time. Life is not fair. Making it someone's fault or finding someone to blame doesn't make unfairness any more pleasant.

As you are going through your day today, determine to strive for fairness in all of your dealings, but accept unfairness with as much grace and dignity as you can muster. Life does, indeed, reward those who make the best of every situation.

Today's the day!

Each year when the calendar rolls over again, human beings all around the world engage in a number of strange behaviors. Many people pass into the new year by consuming entirely too much food and alcohol, then they do the world-famous countdown to the happy new year and begin by sleeping through its first day and suffering the effects of too much food and drink. Then it is time for the annual struggle with New Year's resolutions.

There is something about being forced to write a new year on checks and correspondences that causes people to create absurd resolutions. I have written a number of books dealing with setting goals and reaching life objectives. I am a proponent of making resolutions; however, my method is far different from the haphazard, offhand way people establish New Year's resolutions. Not only do they not work, but they become, in many cases, counterproductive.

Any time we set a goal, we are in essence making a promise to ourselves. If we cannot keep this promise because we were not really serious about the goal in the first place, or if we have set an unrealistic goal, it is that much harder to reach other goals down the road. If you have changes you want to make in your life, or goals you want to begin actively pursuing, January is no better or worse time than any other.

When you do set a goal, whether now or later, be sure it meets the following criteria.

1. Make sure the goal belongs to you. You can't lose weight, quit smoking, or begin being financially responsible because your spouse or mother-in-law thinks you should. The goal must belong to you.

2. Be sure your goal is realistic. Don't set yourself up for failure before you start. Find people who have been successful at reaching the goal you are seeking and follow their pattern.

3. Set a pace that is sustainable. It is much more important to set your sights on what level you will be performing a year from now than trying to overdo it unrealistically today.
4. Enjoy the process. If you are going to be an achiever in this life, you will spend much more time climbing mountains than you will sitting on the peak. Learn to enjoy the road—not only the destination.

Today, resolve either to set a real goal that matters to you or release the baggage of New Year's resolutions.

Today's the day!

In our hectic, fast-paced world, it often seems that we are called upon to do everything better and faster. While performing well is certainly an admirable pursuit, something has to give. I am not now suggesting—nor would I ever suggest—that you ever do less than your best. What I am, instead, suggesting is that we all learn to choose our battles.

Each day we need to focus upon the things that are necessary to move us toward our personal and professional goals. Quite often the things that create stress in our lives are the demands from other people trying to reach their personal or professional goals.

I was told about a plaque on a wall of an upper-level executive assistant that said, "Your current level of stress brought on by your own poor performance or lack of planning is not my problem." While this is intended to be humorous, it does hold within it the ring of truth.

In his landmark book *First Things First,* Dr. Stephen Covey explores the differences between things that are important and things that are urgent. In this world, many things will appear to be urgent because someone is forcing their priorities or deadlines on you. On the other hand, it is rarely critical in a time-management sense to do the important things. Long-range planning, personal development, and professional contacts are all vital to long-term success, but rarely do they carry a sense of urgency that would require you to act upon them today.

When you look at your daily to-do list, try to put it in order as if you were going to get interrupted at some point in the day and not be able to get back to your list. Determine which task is the most important, and do it first. Also, as you are looking at your to-do list, at the end of each task, ask yourself the vital question, "What if I don't?" If there is not a good answer to that question, you should probably eliminate, postpone, or delegate that activity.

Don't get caught up in the twenty-first-century rat race of performing well while doing the wrong things. You get to decide which games you will play and how well you will play them.

Today's the day!

W e live at the most prosperous time in the richest society ever known on the face of the earth. There are more millionaires created each year than in any year previous.

In spite of the doom and gloom from Wall Street, the rich are, indeed, getting richer. Unfortunately, the poor are also getting poorer. The thing that economically has always made our society great is the fact that we have an active and powerful middle class. Many today in the middle class are riding the fence between wealth and poverty. The decisions they make will impact their future and that of their family.

The key to wealth or financial success, surprisingly, is not money. It is, instead, knowledge. If you divided all the money in the world equally among its inhabitants, within a few short years all of that money would find its way back to its current home. Financially successful people reach their goals because they have obtained certain knowledge, and they apply that knowledge daily in their professional and personal finances.

As with any other area of success, if we want to succeed financially we need only follow those successful people who have gone before us. While there are many paths to financial success, there are a few traits that all people who accumulate and maintain wealth possess.

1. You must spend less than you earn, then save and invest the difference. You cannot borrow your way to prosperity. This is the fundamental key to financial success that applies whether you are working for a million dollars a year or for minimum wage. This area of financial management draws more from diet principles than from economic principles. It takes systematic discipline. The get-rich-quick myth is simply a myth.
2. Never borrow money on anything that is declining in value. The combination of interest expense and a declining asset will spell

financial disaster. Unfortunately, this goes against the grain for most people in our society today. Whether cars, clothes, or vacations, these things do not create long-term wealth. The possible exceptions to this rule would include borrowing money for real estate, education, or self-improvement.

3. You must understand and begin to apply the principle of compounding. I would call compounding the Eighth Wonder of the World. Many people understand how this works as relates to Visa and MasterCard, but they have no idea that this same principle can work for them if they will simply save and invest.

When you examine your personal financial goals, there are no right or wrong answers. Money is nothing more than a tool to make your life and that of your family what you want it to be. In the final analysis, money can only buy three things. Money can buy stuff, it can buy memories, and it can buy security. A balance between the three is probably called for when you formulate your own personal and professional financial goals.

Too many people are waiting for their ship to come in, when, in reality, they have never sent a ship out. A little bit of knowledge and discipline is all it will take you to get from here to there.

Today's the day!

Most of the great corporate and family fortunes that have been built in our society have been created utilizing the principle of delayed gratification. Money has been earned, saved, and invested, creating more money being earned, saved, and invested. In the post-World War II era, a new phenomenon became very prevalent. This is known as consumer credit.

Advertisers have told us, "You can have what you want now and pay later." While this is technically true, these advertisers certainly don't tell you the whole story. We have become a society of debtors. Our national, state, and local governments are in debt, so many of us have followed suit and borrowed up to our limits. This is a very worrisome trend as it eliminates the earning, saving, and investing cycle.

Prior to World War II, it was fairly easy to tell prosperous people from working class people; however, the rise of consumer debt and the wide availability of easy credit have given everyone the ability to live "lifestyles of the rich and famous." While there is certainly nothing wrong with living well, I would submit that there is a right way and a wrong way to do it.

If you are mortgaging your future and that of your family for creature comforts or status symbols today, this is a certain road to failure. All we need do to convince ourselves that this trend is pervasive is to examine the plight of our youngest citizens entering the workforce. Recent statistics show that one in five bankruptcies is now being filed by a college student. As someone who graduated from college in the 1980s, I find this astonishing, as most college students then did not even have the ability to get into debt.

Apparently in the new millennium, you can create a massive amount of debt without even having a job or an income of any type. The average college graduate today is carrying $22,800 in student debt and $7,300 in credit card debt. This means that without any income and virtually nothing to show for their spending, average young people are entering into their careers with an excess of $30,000 in debt. This is a staggering number considering it is accumulated before purchasing homes, cars, and other large consumer items.

Remember that no one ever borrowed his or her way to prosperity, whether a government or an individual. If you can't pay for it now, what makes you think you're going to be able to pay for it later? Save and invest. Compounding interest can work as well for you as it does for your credit card company.

Today's the day!

C onventional wisdom teaches us that problems are bad things to be avoided at all costs. While this is true on the surface, problems hold within themselves the keys to great ideas and fabulous opportunities. Once you grasp this concept, you will begin to embrace problems, anticipate problems, and even go out of your way to look for problems.

There are three simple steps to turning your problems into profit.

1. Realize that problems represent opportunities. They represent a new way to think, act, and react. In the past you may have seen a problem as a crisis. The Chinese letter or character for crisis translates to "opportunity on a dangerous wind." The ancient Chinese realized that they could send their small ships out onto the dangerous sea and, while there were problems to be faced, each opportunity lay just beyond that dangerous wind. Once you have recognized a problem that is being experienced by you or someone around you, you are ready to go to the next step.

2. The whole world is looking for a great idea. The only thing you need to do to have a great idea is to wait for a problem to occur, recognize it as a problem, and ask yourself, "How could I have avoided or solved that problem?" The answer to that simple question is a great idea. We must realize that the idea would have never existed without the problem. Herein lies the opportunity. Once we have identified a problem and crafted a solution, we are ready to move toward creating an opportunity.

3. If all you need to do to have a great idea is to find a problem you are experiencing and resolve it, then it holds that all you need to do to have a great business opportunity is ask yourself, "How could I help other people solve or avoid this same problem?" The answer to this question holds the key to great opportunity and

potential profit. Look at every successful product, concept, or business. You will find at their core a product or service that solves people's problems or helps them avoid problems.

Whether it is the automobile, the Internet, or a paperweight, they each in their own way help people to solve or avoid problems. People will pay you great sums of money either individually or collectively once you can identify and solve their problems. No one will ever be more open to your products or services than someone experiencing a problem. If you called on a potential customer at random in order to sell them snow tires, their reactions may range from indifference to downright rejection. On the other hand, if on a snowy winter morning you happen across a motorist who has slid into the ditch, if you can help him get out of the ditch and explain how your snow tires could help him avoid this problem in the future, you will find a very open and willing customer. The more acute and immediate the problem, the more profitable the opportunity becomes.

As you go through your day today, begin to look at problems differently and start turning them into ideas and then profit.

Today's the day!

Everyone who works for a living either is an entrepreneur or works for an entrepreneur. If you work for a small or growing company, this will be obvious to you. If you work for a very large corporation, you may need to take a historical look to understand that the largest multinational organization was once nothing more than an idea in the mind of an entrepreneur. Even if you work for the government, your salary comes from the taxes paid by profitable, hardworking entrepreneurs.

I am very proud to consider myself an entrepreneur, and I have studied the lives and careers of many entrepreneurs throughout the years. Most entrepreneurs are creative, energetic, and focused. They share many consistent traits, but the one factor that is embodied by every entrepreneur is tenacity. Entrepreneurial activity will offer a thousand opportunities to quit. With tenacity, it is impossible to fail. Without it, it is impossible to succeed. The world belongs to the man or woman who simply refuses to quit.

We could put you at the plate in the last game of the World Series and—whether you have ever practiced hitting—I could guarantee your eventual success if we gave you an unlimited number of strikes and you refused to quit.

I have a dear friend who has just started a new business. She is facing that inevitable series of brick walls that all entrepreneurs confront. Her persistence and tenacity make me proud to be her friend.

Whether it is Thomas Edison, Henry Ford, or my friend, the option of quitting has to be ignored, and the opportunity to try again must always be pursued. There is, inevitably, always one more option or avenue to explore. Whether it is in your personal or your professional life, if you think you have thought of everything, you haven't. If you think you've tried it all, you haven't. If you think you've reached the end of your rope, you haven't.

Assume that the solution and the key to your success lie just beyond your next attempt. Your breakthrough is closer than you think.

Today's the day!

S uccess, whether in your personal or your professional life, is a result of making good decisions. Good decisions are a result of gathering all the pertinent information and using good judgment. Good judgment comes from experience, usually the experience of overcoming a problem or a challenge. Too many people rush to a decision or a judgment.

The first thing you need to do when facing any decision is to determine when is the last minute you can finalize your choice without being penalized. Procrastination is rarely considered to be an admirable trait, but when it comes to decision-making, being the first one in line can often hurt you very badly. How often have you heard people who have been the victim of their own poor decision say, "If I had known then what I know now ..."? The reality is that many of these people could have delayed their decision without penalty, and they would have known now that fact or element that they wished they had known earlier.

Once you have determined the last minute you can make your final decision, then you need to start gathering the information you need to know in order to consider all of the alternatives. Let's say you are trying to decide what to wear to work this morning. Obviously, you might listen to the weather report or look out the window. If it's particularly hot or cold, you might want to dress accordingly. If it is raining or snowing, you would want to have an umbrella or boots. This seems elementary, only because you have grown accustomed to having all of the information at your fingertips.

What if I asked you—instead of making a decision today on what you should wear today—to select your wardrobe for a day of work five, six, or seven months in the future? This would be much harder to do, because the information is not available yet. There is no reason you should force yourself into a wardrobe decision months in advance.

Too many people are the victim of bad judgment that results in bad decisions simply because they don't have the information. If they had waited longer to make the decision, this poor outcome could have been avoided.

If you are not sure whether to go right or go left, straddle the fence as long as you can. You may find that both roads merge or that there is a far better alternative road that will present itself a little farther on.

Today's the day!

Do It, Skip It, or Move It

As busy businesspeople pursuing our professional goals and objectives, we are all faced with the inevitable time versus task dilemma. There are more things to do than the time allotted will allow.

One of the greatest factors I find in the amazing success of high-performance individuals is their ability to sift through and categorize potential tasks. Via the mail, telephone, e-mail, or face-to-face meetings, all of us have dozens of opportunities to invest our time every workday. How we invest this time will determine our eventual success or failure.

The old saying "Time is money" still applies. There are more and more people who want to take up your time with their opportunity, their problem, their connection, their crisis. While we certainly want to get involved with those around us, we have to realize that time is a finite commodity. There are many good things to do. Unfortunately, there are not enough hours to do them all, so we must replace the good with the best.

Whenever you are presented with an opportunity to invest your time, you should immediately do one of three things. Do it now, skip it entirely, or move it to a point in the future. Handling paper, e-mail, or telephone interactions one time and immediately is, by far, the most efficient way to conduct your business. Too many people let things pile up on their desk or in their briefcase to be considered later. Much time is wasted by these people simply getting "back up to speed" on the matter at hand. It would have taken no more time or effort to have just handled the issue when it was first presented.

Time is wasted when we are not able to make a decisive decision at that very moment. Therefore, we should: (1) Recognize a task or opportunity as valid and handle it immediately. (2) Recognize it as invalid, a time-waster, or simply something that is not as good as the other things we are pursuing. These items should be eliminated from our landscape. (3) Recognize it as something that is not urgent or immediate but may have some merit. These items should be recorded on our calendar for some future point when we will have more information and either do it, skip it, or move it.

In the business world, much is made of time management. In reality, we cannot manage time. It is a constant force in all of our lives. The only thing we can manage is ourselves and how we choose to invest the time we have been given.

Today's the day!

I n the past several years, there has been an amazing proliferation in the number of consultants, advisers, coaches and mentors. There seems to be any number of people who are willing, for a fee, to tell you and me how to conduct our personal and professional lives. Advice is the quickest way to limit common mistakes, but this same advice will often insure the elimination of undiscovered possibilities.

When considering an adviser, you first have to feel comfortable with their ability and credibility. A few simple rules may be helpful.

1. Never take advice from anybody who doesn't have what you want. They need to be able to demonstrate that they have had success in the critical area you are facing, or they have helped other people in your situation face these critical elements.

2. Never take blanket advice from someone who is selling something or otherwise has a vested interest. Everything is recommended by the guy who is selling it.

3. Make sure your adviser listens a lot before he or she attempts to advise you. It is important they understand fully where you want to go before they tell you how to get there.

4. Whenever possible, pay for results, not advice. If they are willing to make their fee contingent upon your achieving the desired result, you can rest more comfortably.

5. Remember that an adviser can only give you information regarding the known state of the art. Often, your future destiny lies beyond the known universe within your field. Statements such as "It's always been done this way" or "That's never been done before" should be discouraged.

Good advice and counsel come from real-world experience. Never forget that when you are hiring a consultant or adviser, they may have spent many years in the theoretical or academic world while you have been on the front lines obtaining real-world experience. The state of the art, in most arenas, is changing so rapidly that someone who was a worldwide expert ten years ago may now be an obsolete dinosaur.

I like advisers who assume everything is possible and then focus their energy upon how to get from here to there instead of informing me why my ideas or concepts are impractical if not impossible. Advisers are a tool to help you build your dreams, not a critic who will limit them.

Today's the day!

forefront of change. They ushered in a new era. As we look back on them from the perspective of history, we note their single, great accomplishment. But if you will study the details of history, you will realize that every great person through the ages who had a new invention, development, or idea was met with opposition and scorn from those who wanted to maintain the status quo and avoid change.

As you go through your day today, look at each change as an opportunity.

Today's the day!

The Shortcut Myth

All you need to do to convince yourself that our society is addicted to shortcuts to success is to watch late-night cable television. In the brief span of a thirty-minute infomercial, you will be regaled with the supposed merits of wonderful products that will enable you to make millions of dollars instantly, lose fifty pounds by next Tuesday, or meet and marry the person of your dreams before this weekend.

We have become junkies of this shortcut mentality. We regularly watch television shows or movies that present compelling world crises that are resolved within a few minutes or hours, and everyone involved lives happily ever after. Naive people assume that everyone else is already on the fast track, so they are gullible with respect to these shortcut gimmicks.

Beverly Sills, international opera star, noted author, and great patron of the arts, once said, "There are no shortcuts to anywhere worth going." This is true today as it has been true throughout recorded history.

The news is full of stories of people who have experienced "overnight success" in their professional or personal lives. If you will really explore these people's experiences, you will find that their success is a product of many years of focused intensity toward their goals. I would be the first to admit that after many years of focused intensity, success often arrives wrapped in a beautiful package that seems to have been delivered overnight, but, in reality, the success was an intricate recipe that was long in the preparation stage before it came out of the oven.

You may have heard the story of the bamboo trees that grow from a seed and only rise a few inches in the first seven years, then, in that next growing season, they spring up dozens of feet in a miraculous fashion. While it seems all of the growth has happened in a few weeks or months, if you really studied the trees, you would find that for seven years, the root system has been growing and preparing for that one season of rapid growth.

What we call "overnight success" is, most likely, an "overnight discovery" of someone who has been performing at a successful level for quite some time. People who have climbed the corporate ladder have found that the key to success is to perform at the level to which you wish to rise, and then you will be rewarded with that promotion. A promotion is not as much elevating you into a new job as it is recognizing and rewarding the job you have already been doing.

As you go through your day today, be sure that each of the goals you seek are worthy of your talent and efforts, because there is no shortcut from here to there.

Today's the day!

All of us are a part of a team in our professional lives. You may think you are the Lone Ranger or an exception to this rule, but you're not. As I write, it would seem to many that being an author is a one-person job. In reality, I am dictating these words to a very talented person who will then take my words—after she fixes punctuation and grammatical problems I create—and then she will send them to newspapers, magazines, and online publications literally around the globe.

There are other people at each of these sites who make sure they are typeset, printed, loaded into the proper electronic files, etc. In a professional sense, no man or woman is an island. Even if you work alone from your house, you have vendors, suppliers, contractors, as well as customers and clients.

Each of the people on your team must perform well for you to reach your potential. There are several elements to performing well as part of a team.

1. All of the team members must understand their role and how it fits into the overall picture. They must be aware of expectations and deadlines as a part of the overall project or goal.

2. Each individual must understand his or her own personal success as a part of the team experiencing corporate success. An individual football player may perform flawlessly, but without the coordinated efforts of the team, he will suffer failure and defeat.

3. All of the team members must feel that their creativity is appreciated and their input is valued. There may be no better advice on performing a task than that which comes from the individual who constantly performs that single task.

4. Each team member must share in the victory or experience the

defeat. There can be no individual success unless the team succeeds. Every piece of the pie must be valued.

As you go through your day today, consider all of the people on your team that you may have overlooked in the past. Realize that you are only as good as they make you. Understand that the vast majority of people want to be on a winning team, and they want to be a part of something bigger than themselves. Give them a place to fit and a structure where they feel secure and appreciated, and they will make you a superstar.

Today's the day!

THREE KEYS TO THE SALE

In our society, there are relatively few people who would list their profession as salesperson; however, we all succeed or fail on our ability to sell. While we don't all make our living selling goods or services to the general public, each of us has to sell our ideas, our concepts, our abilities, or ourselves in personal and professional situations. A job interview is little more than a sales presentation. You are your own product.

Whether you go to work each day and call on prospects to sell them on your goods and services, chances are you make your living based on a successful sales campaign. To quote an old adage, "Nobody makes any money till somebody sells something." There may be hundreds or even thousands of people supporting that sale, but that salesperson is on the front line, creating the business. It's kind of like Neil Armstrong stepping onto the surface of the moon. While he was the one taking the actual step, there were literally thousands of people who did their part to make that happen and support his efforts.

Selling is the highest-paid profession in the world, and since we all either make our living directly as a salesperson or indirectly in supporting others who are salespeople, it is important that we understand the dynamics.

There are three critical elements that must be present in order to make a win/win sale. A win/win sale is one in which a fair, honest exchange of value is made and both parties benefit. In order for this to happen, you must identify and communicate the following.

1. Interest. The other party must have or must develop an interest in your product or service based on your presentation. This can be as simple as a thirty-second commercial or as complicated as a seven-to-ten contact sales and marketing campaign.

2. Need. The prospects must perceive that they have a need for your

goods or services that is stronger than the need for the money they will spend. The perception of need is more important here than real need. In our society, very few of our purchases are necessities. They are simply things we feel will improve our lives and our image.

3. Resources. The prospects must have the resources to make the purchase you want them to make. No matter how interested they are or how badly they need what you have to sell, unless they have the required price, you are wasting your time and their time.

If you are in the world of selling, be proud of what you do and commit yourself to doing it well. If you are not directly involved in sales on a daily basis, find those people in your organization who are, and then support their efforts and encourage their success. When salespeople succeed, we all succeed.

Today's the day!

TRAINING

We have heard it said a thousand times that practice makes perfect. As well meaning as the person who told you this might have been, he was wrong. Practice does not make perfect. Practice makes consistent. Perfect practice makes perfect. Mediocre practice makes mediocrity.

One of the things sadly lacking in today's professional business environment is training. What they call training is more often a partial transfer of information that rapidly forces the new person into overload.

I believe that the food-service industry does a better job of training than most other sectors. How many times have you gone into a restaurant and been approached by not one, but two waiters or waitresses? Then they immediately inform you that one is training the other, or the new person is "mirroring" one of the experienced waitstaff. The management in the food-service industry understands that nothing provides training like hands-on experience in real-life situations.

Some of the most successful coaches in sports understand this as well. They will try to do everything possible to simulate game conditions. They try to practice at the same time of day that the game will be played, and they often pipe in recorded crowd noise at the level that can be expected during the real game. They understand that it's quite different to carry out a play well on a quiet, familiar court or playing field. It's quite another thing to perform well under loud, confused, and unfamiliar conditions. Nothing takes the place of real-world experience.

If you are learning a new skill or profession, try to find realistic conditions and turn them into learning experiences. If you are in charge of training others, create simulations in ways that people can learn their new skills without risking poor performance. Back to our friends in the food-service industry. It's one thing to have a brand-new waiter or waitress serving a valuable customer with an experienced waitstaff by their side to observe and step in if necessary. It's quite another thing to risk a valued customer with someone who has had nothing but an employee's manual to read and learn from.

As you go through your day today, find safe, realistic experiences to learn from and to teach those around you how to perform at the highest possible level.

Today's the day!

W e live in a world that in a few short decades has gone from "a person's word is their bond" to "you can't believe anything you hear." In the course of one day in my office, via e-mail, fax, and unsolicited phone calls, I will be told that I have qualified for a $99.00 all-inclusive trip to Disney World; I may already have won $10 million; if I will order computer supplies, I will be given a free computer; a salesman wants to stop by for no more than ten minutes to bring me a free gift; and dozens of other dubious offers. It has reached a point that, mentally, everything we are told is discounted and diluted to such an extent that it is virtually meaningless.

It is ironic that while trying to dictate this very column, I was interrupted by a phone call that I was forced to take because a rude woman insisted that it was regarding a lost or stolen credit card. My assistant put the call through to me; however, in reality, the woman was trying to sell me a credit card protection package that, according to her, would protect me if and when my credit card was lost or stolen.

If you can't believe people during the introduction or initial meeting, why would you ever want to have a personal or professional relationship with them? How can you ever trust anything they tell you? Whatever happened to undersell and overdeliver?

One of my mentors told me when I was in my early twenties that the key to success in business is to always do what you say you are going to do. First, this will give you a reputation for honesty and integrity. Second, and maybe more importantly, if you know you are going to have to follow through on everything you say, you will be much more careful and cautious with what you promise.

As we all know, if something seems too good to be true, it probably is. There are people asking you to give them your money, your support, and your votes. These people want you to trust them to lead us into a troubled future, and they tell us with a straight face that they are going to lower taxes, cut spending, and increase services and benefits for everyone.

As you go through your day today, look for people who do what they say they are going to do. Allow them into your inner circle and reject everyone else. You will have a wonderful day and a wonderful life.

Today's the day!

In human terms, a century seems like an eternity, but in historical terms, it is little more than the blink of an eye. An ancient blessing from father to son says, "May you live in interesting times." My dear reader, you and I do, indeed, live in interesting times. Let's turn back the calendar, a historical blink of an eye, to 1904. Let's see what the world looked like four years after the turn of the last century. Keep in mind that there are people alive and well today who were already born in 1904. People over 100 years of age are the fastest-growing segment of our population.

In 1904, only 14 percent of the homes in the United States had a bathtub. Only 8 percent of the homes had a telephone. A three-minute call from Denver to New York City cost eleven dollars. There were only eight thousand cars in the United States, and only 144 miles of paved roads. The maximum speed limit in most cities was ten miles per hour. Alabama, Mississippi, Iowa, and Tennessee were each more heavily populated than California. With a mere 1.4 million residents, California was only the twenty-first most populous state in the Union. The tallest structure in the world was the Eiffel Tower.

The average wage in the United States was twenty-two cents an hour. The average U.S. worker made between $200 and $400 per year. A competent accountant could expect to earn $2,000 per year, a dentist $2,500 per year, a veterinarian between $1,500 and $4,000 per year, and a mechanical engineer about $5,000 per year. More than 95 percent of all births in the United States took place at home. Ninety percent of all U.S. physicians had no college education. Instead, they attended medical schools, many of which were condemned in the press and by the government as "substandard." The average life expectancy was forty-seven years.

Sugar cost four cents a pound. Eggs were fourteen cents a dozen.

Coffee was fifteen cents a pound. Most women only washed their hair once a month, and used borax or egg yolks for shampoo. Canada passed a law prohibiting poor people from entering the country for any reason. The five leading causes of death in the United States were pneumonia and influenza; tuberculosis; diarrhea; heart disease; and stroke.

The American flag had forty-five stars. Arizona, Oklahoma, New Mexico, Hawaii, and Alaska hadn't been admitted to the Union yet. The population of Las Vegas, Nevada, was thirty. Crossword puzzles, canned beer, and iced tea hadn't been invented. There was no Mother's Day or Father's Day. Two of ten American adults couldn't read or write. Only 6 percent of all Americans had graduated high school. Marijuana, heroin, and morphine were all available over-the-counter at corner drugstores. According to one pharmacist, "Heroin clears the complexion, gives buoyancy to the mind, regulates the stomach and bowels, and is, in fact, a perfect guardian of health." Eighteen percent of households in the United States had at least one full-time servant or domestic. There were only about 230 reported murders in the entire United States.

What a difference a century makes. As you go through your day today, think of things you can do with your life that will make a difference in the world a century from now.

Today's the day!

HIRING AND FIRING YOURSELF

One of the most prominent facets of what we call the great American dream is the notion of working for yourself. Controlling your own destiny has an allure like few other ideas. In reality, all of us who are employed, to a great extent, work for ourselves.

You may have a job in the middle of a flowchart in a giant corporate or government bureaucracy, but you still, in essence, work for yourself. Earning money is the key indicator of your success in working for yourself. Only people who work in the mint make money. The rest of us earn money. This is simply a function of creating more value than you are paid. As your value increases, your pay should increase. You can give yourself a raise by simply continuing to increase your value far beyond the point where you are paid. Eventually, your pay will catch up to your value.

Supply and demand is such that if you are in an organization that does not appreciate, recognize, or reward your value, another organization will seek you out if you continue to increase your value. A wise person once told me that no one gets fired. They fire themselves. While I understand the reality of economic downturns and layoffs, this statement is still true in that those people who have created the most value seem to always have a job in an exciting, growing field where they are adequately compensated.

Look at yourself and your job as a one-person corporation. What can you do to be more efficient and increase the contribution you make to the larger organization? People are rewarded for solving problems. They are even more highly rewarded for anticipating problems and heading them off before they occur.

As you go through your day today, assess the value of your one-person corporation in light of how much you are paid. Look for ways to increase your value and the unique contributions you make to everyone within your organization. This level of personal commitment is contagious. Once you begin to increase your value, those around you will follow suit. As this tide of success comes in, all the boats will be lifted—including yours.

Today's the day!

It is ironic that the people who most need to receive a message are often those least likely to hear it. Too often, we are a good judge of everyone's character except our own. Unfortunately, we view everyone else in light of their results but view ourselves based on our good intentions. If you can find a few people in your personal and professional life who will be honest with you about your own performance, you are, indeed, fortunate. The most valuable people on any team are those who will be frank and honest with the leader.

There are two basic kinds of leaders—those who lead by fear and those who lead by respect. In the short run, both methods will appear to work; however, the only long-term fuel that will propel a team to greatness is respect. You have probably heard about the old sign that was posted on a job site so that all the workers saw it daily. "Firings will continue until morale improves." While this will generate a great deal of activity, it will not improve productivity. In fact, fear is the least effective long-term human motivator.

People who fear for their jobs and careers will do the least they can to stand out from the crowd. If you lead by fear, you will get the letter of what you asked for but not the spirit of what you need. In order to get your team's honesty, creativity, and maximum efforts, you must lead from respect. The only way to get your team members to respect you is to demonstrate to them on a daily basis that you respect them.

At the point you are forced to deal with someone in your personal or professional life in the context of fear, you have already lost the battle and are on the verge of losing the war. Most people on a team want to perform at a high level. They feel the peer pressure of those around them and the momentum that teamwork creates. Threats of being fired or otherwise disciplined, except in extreme cases, take away all of that positive momentum and leave the team in confusion and fear.

People who are afraid quit thinking about their goals and start thinking about the consequences. There's a big difference between succeeding and not failing. People who want to succeed will join hands with everyone on the team and multiply their efforts. On a good team, one plus one equals three. On a team full of fear one plus one equals one-and-a-half. People will point fingers and blame one another instead of solving problems and reaching the goal.

You have probably seen a basketball team enjoying a twenty-point lead, trying to hold the ball and run out the clock. This strategy quite often fails because teams are built for success and winning, not holding the ball in an attempt to not lose. As you go through your day today, respect those around you, and you will find a team worthy of any task before you.

Today's the day!

Those of us who are blessed to live in a free society as we enter into the twenty-first century owe a great debt to a handful of people who led us through the first half of the last century. Among these people to whom we are indebted is certainly Winston Churchill. He led with his words, his deeds, and—most importantly—his character. The mere power of his presence and his persona emboldened allies fighting for freedom all around the globe. He may be among the most quoted people in recorded history.

I believe Churchill would have been considered great if he had lived at any other time in the past; however, as stated by one of my favorite authors, Louis L'Amour, "A person can only be judged based on the backdrop of the time and place in which they live." Churchill was a decisive, powerful force at the time in history when a decisive, powerful person was most needed. He had the gift of having something significant to say and, just as importantly, he had the gift of being able to say it in a way that others could internalize.

In one of my favorite Churchill quotes, he leaves us to ponder, "Success is never final. Failure is never fatal. It is courage that counts." In this thought, Churchill reminds us that our success or failure is merely what we do or what we have done, but our character is who we are. Too often, those who have had temporary success stop progressing because they see this brief success as a destination instead of a springboard to greater things. Often, those who have suffered a temporary setback see it as a life sentence that they must live with. In reality, where we have been is mostly irrelevant if we have a firm understanding of where we are going and how we are going to get there.

Churchill understood that today's headlines are tomorrow's

memories. We always have the opportunity to build on success or reverse failure. We are not our performance. Instead, we are our character. If you will focus on becoming the person you want to be, success and failure will take care of themselves. Great people will always do great things.

Today's the day!

The only meaningful advice you will ever hear about investing tells you to "buy low, sell high." The thousands of books that have been written about investing are designed based on a number of theories as to how to do that; but at the end of the day, the objective is still to buy low, sell high. If it is so simple, why do so many people fail in investing and in life? They don't fail because they don't know what to do. They fail because they don't do what they know.

Too many people make their investments and are committed to hold them for a number of years; but then they open a newspaper or watch a television report that tells them the market is bad, and they panic. They end up buying high and selling low, even though they know better. When they invested, they knew intellectually that there would be times the market would be up just as there would be times the market would be down.

The only long-term wisdom is to trust in the fact that, over the long haul, the market will always trend upward. It's as if we were watching a young boy walk up the stairs while he is playing with a yo-yo. If you keep your eye on the yo-yo, it will be bouncing up and down and cause you to panic. If you simply watch the overall direction of the boy, you will stay calm and ultimately be successful. Success in investing and in life depends on sticking with your plan in spite of current circumstances.

Recently, I heard about an employer who hired a qualified, energetic candidate. Shortly after this new employee started work, he made a costly mistake that caused the employer to lose thousands of dollars. The new employee nervously asked his employer, "Are you going to fire me?" The employer wisely responded, "No, I'm not going to fire you. I hired the best candidate I could and, besides that, I have just invested thousands of dollars in your education."

Stick with your best plans that lead you toward your best goals and objectives. The best plans and strategies occasionally look bad in the short term but succeed in the long term. Hold on through the tough times, and you will sell high in your investments, in your career, and your life.

Today's the day!

There is an old saying that goes, "Millionaires are different from the rest of us." This is not true. Millionaires are just like everyone else with one exception. They think differently. They have a unique perspective on business, money, and success that has made them millionaires. They do not have this unique perspective because they are rich. They are rich because they have this unique perspective.

The key to wealth is not money but knowledge. If you took all the money in the world and divided it evenly among everyone, within a few short years, the previous millionaires would be wealthy once again. If you want to be a millionaire, you've got to begin to think like a millionaire in the following ways.

1. Millionaires understand that people don't make money unless they work in a mint. Everyone else has to earn money.

2. Millionaires understand that there is generally no way to get rich quick. Look for Crock-Pot solutions, not microwave solutions.

3. Millionaires learn how, at every level, to live on less than they earn so that their money can begin working for them instead of them working for their money.

4. Millionaires understand the difference between cost and value. This is an anticonsumer mentality. Millionaires want to know that when they convert their dollars to things, those things retain their value.

5. Millionaires seek advice from the best professionals available and from millionaire mentors. They only get advice from people who have what they want.

6. Millionaires march to their own drummer and seek their own goals. They really don't care who is or is not impressed by them.

7. Millionaires understand what money will do and will not do. Money will buy things, security, or memories, but it will not make you happy.

8. Millionaires understand the equation between time and money. Money is in abundant supply in the marketplace. Time can never be replaced; therefore, millionaires will trade reasonable amounts of money to save their time.

9. Millionaires are, by and large, self-made. Over 80 percent of millionaires are first generation. They generally want their heirs to have the same experiences they had in struggling, earning, and creating wealth.

10. Millionaires use their money and enjoy people instead of those shallow individuals who try to use people and enjoy money. Money can be replaced. People cannot.

As you go through your day today, begin to think like a millionaire, and then you will begin to act like a million. Before you know it, you will be a millionaire.

Today's the day!

KEEPING IT TO YOURSELF

We all have problems, challenges, anxieties, and fears that we deal with in our personal as well as our professional lives. This is to be expected. One of the biggest questions in how we deal with our challenges is, who do we tell?

Regarding the sharing of problems, people seem to fall into one of two extreme categories. There are people who want to share every problem about everything with everyone they encounter, and then to the other extreme there are people who silently face everything alone and won't share anything with anyone. Invariably, both extreme approaches lead to personal and professional failure.

Those who have a tendency to tell everyone everything minimize their own credibility. They want to tell everyone "The sky is falling" so often they become like the little boy "crying wolf." If you can stand the two fairy-tale analogies in one sentence, you will realize that making a public broadcast of every challenge and problem in your life diminishes you. We become known to those around us based on how we handle challenges and immediate problems. On the other hand, if you decide to tell no one and go it alone, you cut off all potential sources of advice, support, and encouragement. When you really do have serious challenges, there are many people around you who want to be a part of your solution.

Before you share your personal or professional problems, fears, concerns, or challenges with others, you might want to first answer the following questions.

1. Is this a real problem or is it simply a minor annoyance that is a standard part of life?
2. Am I telling this person for a productive, constructive reason or am I just spreading misery?
3. Is this a person who can possibly bring advice, support, or encouragement to my situation?

4. Do I have all of the facts, or am I reacting prematurely?

If you can answer each of these questions favorably, it is probably in your best interest to take a handful of trusted friends or colleagues into your confidence as it relates to your current problems or challenges. On the other hand, if you cannot answer all the questions favorably, you will probably be better off simply keeping it to yourself. There is nothing more powerful than sharing a burden with someone who cares and is willing and able to help. And there are few things more destructive than sharing your doubts and fears with someone who doesn't care or is not in a position to make a difference.

As you go through your day today, resolve to manage your problems and challenges without letting them manage you.

Today's the day!

P art of the great American dream for many people is to own their own business. I am often asked, "What must people do to become a successful entrepreneur?" The answer is quite a challenge, because I have seen people start and run successful businesses doing everything you can imagine and some things you cannot imagine.

So, as often happens, the best way to answer this question and the best way to succeed, is simply to avoid failure. Entrepreneurs fail for a number of reasons, and if these can be avoided, success moves from possible to probable and becomes likely. Here are five principles that can help the would-be entrepreneur avoid failure.

1. Entrepreneurs must examine the three "Ts"—time, temperament, and talent. You must honestly assess yourself or, better yet, have friends, colleagues, and family members who know you best help you. I have seen people who have a sixty-hour-a-week "day job" who coach the Little League team and are on the PTA but feel they have enough *time* to start a new business. As many ventures are begun part time, you must be realistic about how much time you have to invest. Second, our own *temperament* is difficult for us to evaluate because, in our own mind, we always act logically and reasonably. You must ask people with whom you have worked if you really have the temperament to be in business for yourself. The third "T" is *talent*. It is very easy to underestimate the talent it takes to create a new venture, because talented people by their very nature make everything look easy. Michael Jordan and Tiger Woods seem effortless when they are at their best. But don't underestimate their level of talent.

2. Find your market niche. The whole key to entrepreneurship is to find a need and fill it. You must assess if there is really a demand

for your product or service. You may love chocolate-chip waffles or tofu bagels, but is the world ready for these new products?

3. Make sure you have enough capital. The cardinal sin in operating a business is to run out of money. Money smooths the highway before you and helps you overcome mistakes. If you don't have enough operating capital, you may have to do everything perfectly the first time. This simply never works.

4. Get out of the corporate mentality. Many would-be entrepreneurs come out of midlevel corporate America. They have had tremendous advantages due to the resources of their employer. These advantages will simply not be there in a start-up venture. In the corporate world, your assistant may have an assistant, but in Entrepreneurland, get ready to do it yourself.

5. Don't underestimate the amount of work and passion required. Starting a business may be the hardest, most difficult, and most rewarding thing you do. Many sacrifices will have to be made—particularly in the beginning. If you don't have the passion for your new venture, or if you have grossly underestimated the work required, you'll never make it.

If you can avoid these pitfalls and you have a product, service, or concept that the marketplace wants, I would encourage you to begin now and simply never quit.

Today's the day!

BIG PICTURE VERSUS DETAILS

In any venture or enterprise, you need two separate and distinct thought patterns. You must consider the big picture, and you must consider the details. Many big-picture thinkers do not understand the importance of details, and many meticulous detail thinkers fail to understand the vital nature of the big picture.

Without details and follow-through, a big-picture or great idea is simply a fantasy. It will never be brought to reality without attention to specific tasks, deadlines, and follow-through. On the other hand, outstanding attention to detail will go nowhere without the direction provided by big-picture thinking. This is like a well-tuned car that has been meticulously maintained setting out without a road map or destination.

One of my cherished friends and colleagues, Dr. Robert Schuller, often says, "Don't get the 'how you are going to do it' mixed up in the 'what are you going to do' phase." Dr. Schuller means that you should never limit your goal-setting or planning based on your current understanding of what is feasible. If you limit your destination to your current knowledge, you will probably never build a Crystal Cathedral like Dr. Schuller did. On the other hand, even someone like Dr. Schuller, who is one of the biggest-picture thinkers I know, would never begin to build a Crystal Cathedral or even finalize plans for such an undertaking without architects, engineers, and detail people who can direct the project.

Often, the two schools of thought seem to be at odds. Big-picture thinkers see opportunities and possibilities far into the future and do not often consider the practical aspects of the undertaking. Detail people often identify every problem and obstacle without considering the value of the goal. Only when the two mind-sets come together can you safely and effectively reach your maximum potential.

I am very grateful to work in an environment where I have the freedom to express grandiose and often outlandish thoughts and ideas. I am also grateful to work in an environment where I am surrounded by the best detail people I have ever met. I always want to be sure that they can deliver what I promise.

As you go through your day today, either consider each opportunity from both a big-picture and a detail perspective or find someone in your world who will bring the missing element to the planning and implementation process. When you do this, you will definitely find out that two heads are better than one.

Today's the day!

I am a big proponent of continuing education and personal development. As the author of a dozen books and hundreds of columns, and as a success speaker at numerous arena and convention events, I believe in learning everything possible; however, when it's all said and done, unfortunately there's a lot more said than done. When we fail in business or in life, we don't fail because we don't know what to do; we fail because we don't do what we know.

From time to time, it's good to get a check up on the very basic business success principles that we all know but few of us apply on a regular basis. Consider the following:

1. Is your telephone answered politely and professionally, identifying in an understandable fashion whom the caller has reached?

2. Do you promptly and professionally correspond and communicate with your clients and prospects?

3. Do you thank your existing customers for the business they have given you thus far?

4. Do you express appreciation and gratitude to employees, coworkers, and colleagues who make your success possible?

5. Are you constantly reading business books, success articles, and attending industry presentations that will keep you on the cutting edge of success?

6. Do you set aside time regularly for medium- and long-range planning, or are you caught up in always putting out today's fires?

7. Have you surrounded yourself with the very best CPAs, attorneys, financial planners, computer techs, and other individuals who will help you build on your success?

8. Are you scheduling time off for recreation, family time, and other activities essential to having a balanced life and a refreshed attitude?

9. Do you constantly set new goals for yourself and individuals within your organization so that there is always a challenge in front of everyone?
10. Do you give back to your community, your industry, and those around you who may need a helping hand? You didn't get there on your own. They won't either.

These are ten simple ideas that any elementary school student studying business would readily understand. There is nothing revolutionary or earth-shattering among these thoughts, but if you regularly apply these things that you already know, you will become a legend in your industry and a success far beyond your wildest dreams.

As you go through your day today, continue to gain new knowledge, but don't forget to practice the things you already know.

Today's the day!

The Contract Concept

A lot of time, effort, energy, and money is spent creating, organizing, changing, executing, and disputing contracts. For better or worse, contracts and the legal problems that surround them have become a permanent part of our lives. You may have heard it said that a contract is not worth the paper it is written on. In some cases, this can be true, and in other cases, a contact may be worth many times its weight in gold. In a perfect world, I prefer to think of a contract as a memory tool between two honorable parties.

Considering the pace at which we conduct business in the twenty-first century, it is difficult to remember what you did this morning, much less the terms and conditions you committed to months or even years ago. A properly constructed and executed contract can take both parties back to the time and place of an agreement. A contract should, ideally, address every contingency and totally reflect both parties' intentions.

In order to have both parties uphold a contract, there must be two elements present on each side of the agreement. These two elements are willingness and ability. You could have had a mutually agreeable binding contract with a firm in New Orleans to deliver certain products or services to you. This organization may have had the best of intentions and been totally willing to fulfill the contract, but then along comes Hurricane Katrina, and they are simply unable to live up to their agreement. Whether by acts of nature, financial reversals, or other outside elements, ability to perform under a contract can be greatly affected. Through insurance and other means, the ability portion of risk can be generally handled and protected with a well-written contract.

The willingness of a party to be honorable and perform under a contact is a much more difficult and troublesome element of the agreement. If we understand that a contract is a memory tool between honorable parties, the contract becomes worthless if one party remembers the commitment but is simply not willing to perform as committed. In this case, the contract is, indeed, "not worth the paper it is written on."

If everyone had a perfect memory and was totally honorable, a simple handshake agreement would be more than enough for every transaction. Conversely, if you are dealing with dishonorable parties, an airtight contract the size of a phone book may not protect you, or if it does protect you, the legal costs of sustaining your position may simply be more than it is worth.

As you go through your day today, endeavor to have solid contracts but, more importantly, make sure you're dealing with solid people.

Today's the day!

THE COST OF EMPLOYEES

If you're in charge of an organization or in charge of a team of people within an organization, it is critical that you understand the true cost and value of employees. The cost of an employee, as any business owner will tell you, goes far beyond the salary or hourly wage. Taxes, benefits, insurance plans, sick days, vacation time, and so many other elements enter into the equation. A good employee is worth his or her weight in gold, and a bad employee becomes a black hole that sucks effort and energy out of your universe.

If you are in charge of people, you are like a good coach. You've got to have the right people in the right place at the right time doing the right thing for the right reason. If these elements are out of alignment, your effectiveness as a leader and your staff's effectiveness as employees fall off geometrically. If you have the wrong person doing the wrong thing, your cost-to-reward ratio can be totally out of proportion.

Michael Jordan, while playing basketball, was probably among the most cost-effective employees any organization ever had. Jordan attracted so much revenue to his organization while he was on the basketball court that he affected his team and the entire league. However, if you had taken Michael Jordan in his prime and moved him from the basketball floor to the concession stand in the arena, no matter how great a job he did in manning the concession stand, he could never be worth even a fraction of his salary to the organization.

Most organizations have a mission statement. The purpose of this statement is to reflect the goals and objectives of the organization. Many times, these mission statements are created by people totally removed from the employees charged with the responsibility of reaching the mission. When people are responsible for a goal that they are unable to relate to, you get an organizational and individual disconnect.

Ideally, every person within an organization's personal goals combined with everyone else's personal goals should collectively add up to the mission statement of the organization. If the salespeople's production goals and the creative team's image goals along with the manufacturing or service group's goals for output all come together, it should look like the overall objective of the corporation. Unfortunately, too many organizations have never even thought of the employees as individuals and what mission statements they might have in mind for their own lives and how that might play into the organization's objectives.

As you go through your day today, look at every employee as an investment and determine how you can make that investment more valuable for the organization and that employee.

Today's the day!

C lear, accurate, and concise communication is the key to success in your personal or professional life. I have found over the years that everything is clear to me in my mind. Unfortunately, problems arise when I forget that the thoughts in my mind may or may not be clear to someone else.

Recently, we put a small theater in our office so we could review movies and television shows that we have worked on and screen videos of presentations I have made onstage at corporate or arena events. Our team put a lot of planning into how we would set up the theater and how we would use it. To meet decor and soundproofing needs, we needed to have one entire long wall of floor-to-ceiling drapery. Since it would require nearly ten-foot drapes, I was told that we would need to have custom ones made, as ten-foot drapes are not standard.

A woman was referred to us, and we met with her regarding the project. We ordered a great quantity of material and when the shipment arrived, we gave the bolts of cloth to the drape woman so she could begin work. Several weeks later, she installed the drapes and then invited our team into the theater to examine her work. Everyone was in shock, as the drapes were a different color than the material we had purchased. On further examination, it was determined that she had made these drapes using the back instead of the front of the fabric.

This created a great deal of turmoil. Then it occurred to me that while we had discussed all of the measurements, delivery dates, and costs, surrounding the project, we had never actually confirmed which side of the material would be used. We had assumed since we had purchased the material from a sample that it should be obvious that the side of the fabric shown in the sample was the front. The drape woman, for reasons of her own, decided the other side of the material was the front.

While there may be no right or wrong regarding the material, there was a serious problem. The problem was not which side of the material to use or what looked better. The problem was we had not communicated, so both parties had assumed that a critical element of the project was clear when it obviously wasn't. There are no details too small to clarify, and double-checking is always faster and easier than repairing damage and starting over.

As you go through your day today, take every opportunity to communicate clearly. At worst, you will be considered to be a detail-oriented professional. At best, you will save a lot of pain and suffering.

Today's the day!

All of us in business deal with an amazing array of numbers. Our accountants provide us with facts, figures, and percentages that are beyond most of our abilities to comprehend. Generally, everyone in business understands two numbers: the top line and the bottom line. The top line represents everything we sell, market, and bring in to our operation. The bottom line represents what is left over after we pay all our expenses out of the top-line figure. In order to increase our profitability, we have to do one of two things: Either bring in more business to the top line or spend less before we get to the bottom line.

While this seems to be an irrefutable law of business, there are rare times when it is best to actually cut your top line. At least, temporarily. If you will look at all of your clients, accounts, or customers and then think of all of the problems and crises you have experienced in the last year, you may determine that virtually all of your headaches are coming from one or two customers. Often, these customers are not that significant to your top line, and they are costing you money before they get to your bottom line.

We all deal with our competition, and this is healthy; however, there are some problem customers you would actually be well advised to give to your competition. It may be your fault, it may be your customer's fault, or it may be a number of unavoidable intangibles, but there are occasions when you simply can't please one or two customers. On these occasions, it would be best to politely and professionally let them know that you want to help them transition their business to someone else.

If your customer is not happy, they are not providing profit, motivation, or referrals to your company. In fact, they may be creating so many problems that need correction that you are losing money and frustrating everyone on your team while having a dissatisfied customer telling everyone that you provide poor service. It would be much better to release this customer and fill their slot with a new, satisfied, profitable customer. It is very hard to do this, as we all have been indoctrinated into the belief that clients are good, and more clients are even better.

As you go through your day today, you may actually need to take one step backward by releasing an unprofitable customer in order to take two steps forward by creating new opportunities with future customers.

Today's the day!

SALES AND MARKETING

ales and *marketing* are two terms that are often heard together and even used interchangeably. They are both vital to success but are two extremely different, sometimes opposite, concepts. The terms *import* and *export* are also used together, but as you know, they are quite opposite when you consider any transaction.

Sales, for the sake of this discussion, is the process of contacting potential buyers to present your products or services. Marketing, on the other hand, is the process of creating an environment where potential consumers call you about your product or service. While the desired result may be the same, the process and skill set required are totally different.

One of the salesperson's first tasks in any communication is to demonstrate a need for the product or service to be offered. The person selling insurance, for example, would contact you, informing you of the risk and peril you are in if you do not have insurance. While this is honorable, valid, and sometimes effective, it can be much more desirable when the perspective customer, through marketing efforts, becomes aware of the need for insurance and initiates the communication.

Sales and marketing create two totally different emotional dynamics in the mind of the potential customer. Consider the difference of two phone conversations.

1. You are sitting at home relaxing after a hard day's work, preparing to enjoy a family dinner, when the phone rings. It is a fast-talking, high-pressure salesperson calling you about a vacation opportunity of a lifetime. Your immediate reaction is total resistance and a desire to get off the phone as quickly as possible.

2. You are relaxing around the dinner table with the family after a hard day's work. The topic of a summer vacation comes up and

various family members begin excitedly discussing their ideas for a trip. Then someone remembers an advertisement, flyer, or magazine article, and you pick up the phone and call a resort to get information and make a reservation.

In both cases, you are on the phone with a representative of a vacation company; however, the dynamic is totally different because one is an imposition and the other is fulfilling a need or desire you have identified yourself. This need or desire may have been created by an effective marketing campaign, but in any event, it has set the stage for the sales process.

Sales and marketing are both effective tools in much the same way that a hammer and a screwdriver are both useful but hardly interchangeable.

As you go through your day today, look at your efforts in sales and marketing. Determine to understand the differences and do both well.

Today's the day!

There are four clear states of knowledge and understanding in which you can find yourself.

1. You know something and know that you know it.
2. You know something, but you don't know you know it.
3. You don't know something, but you don't know that you don't know it.
4. You don't know something, but you know that you don't know it.

All of us live part of our personal or professional lives in each of these areas at one time or another. They each have their advantages and disadvantages. If you know something and know that you know it, you can act with confidence and profit from the experience; however, it is important to not rest in this knowledge as the state of the art will always change, and the rate of change is accelerating daily. People who know a computer program and know that they know it will be forced to upgrade their skills as new generations of software are developed, or they will be left behind.

All of us, from time to time, know something but don't know that we know it. This is caused by a lack of perspective. There is probably a piece of property near where you live that you have driven by countless times. Then, all of a sudden, it becomes extremely valuable and is developed in such a way that the owners or speculators profit greatly. If you will look back at the situation, you may realize that, had you thought about it from a different perspective, you knew—or at least should have known—that that property would increase in value. You simply didn't compile the knowledge in such a way that you could recognize the value and act upon it.

The most dangerous people in the world are those who don't know something, but they don't realize that they don't know it. These are the people who go through life and fall into every pitfall and obstacle along the way. They think they know it all, but in reality, they only learn from the mistakes that their ignorance causes them to make. They are over-confident, and you simply can't tell them anything. The best you can do for them is to stand back and help pick them up after the inevitable crash and burn.

The greatest potential is held by those people who don't know something but understand that they don't know it. This is a powerful concept in that they can understand that there is something they don't know and recognize that they need to know it. These individuals rarely make mistakes, and they are always growing and developing. The world doesn't belong to them yet, but it probably will someday.

As you go through your day today, act on the things you know and build on the things you don't know.

Today's the day!

From an early age, we are encouraged by friends, relatives, and those who care about us to "be careful," "take it easy," and "watch out." The thinking behind these admonitions is that we've got to avoid dangerous situations and eliminate risk in our lives. It is certainly prudent to avoid exposing ourselves to unnecessary danger; however, the idea of eliminating risk is counterproductive. Risk is all around us. It invades every area of our personal and professional lives. There is a false assumption that one choice carries risk with it while the alternative choice is risk free.

In the investment world, the riskiest investments are considered to be real estate and the stock market, while guaranteed bank or government accounts are considered the safest investments. While the bank and government investments do guarantee that you will not lose your money, over the last fifty years they have proven to be the most dangerous and risk-laden decisions you could have made.

While the stock market and real estate invariably go up and down, at times reminiscent of a roller coaster, over the long haul they have consistently performed well and offered good investment returns. On the other hand, over the same half-century, the "safe and conservative" investments, which are guaranteed by banks or the government, have not even kept up with inflation; therefore, they inevitably lose value.

Prudent financial advisers will tell you that there is a place for all kinds of investments. I would certainly agree; however, the point we want to understand is that risk and safety rarely are easily identified and totally pure.

I know people who are afraid to fly, so they drive on cross-country trips. Their fear, obviously, is that they could be a victim of a plane crash if they fly on an airplane. While this is statistically possible, the risk of dying in a plane crash is insignificant compared to the risk of driving your own vehicle. In reality, more people are injured or killed driving to the airport than on a commercial airliner.

Every successful business began adrift in a sea of risk. There were a multitude of things that could go wrong for every one that could go right. Many start-up ventures fail, but a few grow, prosper, and eventually succeed. The only way to guarantee failure in a business venture is never to begin. If you launch your dream, you might fail. If you never start, you are guaranteed to fail.

As you go through your day today, reexamine risk and safety. Never take a risk you don't have to, but never play it safe when it guarantees your failure.

Today's the day!

Conversations are pleasant, discussions are interesting, debates are productive, but arguments are destructive. The difference between debates and arguments lies in whether you are dealing with the subject at hand or the personalities involved.

Whether in your personal or professional life, you will inevitably encounter a difference of opinion. This is not a bad thing. In fact, if you don't frequently encounter a difference of opinion, then you have no opinion, the people around you have no opinion, or people are not feeling the freedom to express themselves. In any event, conversation, discussion, and debate are positive. They can ignite people's passions, their creativity, and bring their best ideas to the table; however, once it descends into an argument, there is a lot to be lost and little, if anything, to be gained.

Often, colleagues are put in a position to express differing opinions. There is a right way and a wrong way to carry on these dialogues. Here are a few rules for keeping your conversation on a positive plane.

1. Be sure the time is appropriate for a debate. Don't hijack people in the hall or catch someone rushing off to another commitment. Be sure there is time for a productive discussion.

2. Be sure that the setting is conducive to a good conversation. It should take place where all of the relevant parties can comfortably come together, and interruptions should be avoided. Whenever possible, noninvolved parties should be excluded.

3. Everyone should agree on the matter to be discussed. Whenever possible, only one subject should be tackled at a time. Everyone should agree on what is being decided, when the decision needs to be made, and what factors are involved in coming to a positive resolution.

4. Only one person should talk at a time. Interruptions are

threatening and counterproductive when people are expressing opposite opinions. If necessary, establish a "magic pen," which is passed around from person to person as he or she speaks. No one is allowed to talk unless he or she hold the "magic pen."

5. Agree that appropriate language will be used, everyone will be treated with respect, and the voice level will not be raised. If someone inadvertently violates this rule, calmly point it out and get back to the subject at hand.

6. Find out not only what people who oppose you feel, but also why they believe their position is best. Try to understand their position so you can repeat their argument to them. This will demonstrate respect and create clarity.

Remember, in an argument, there are only losers. In a productive debate or discussion, everyone can win.

As you go through your day today, find ways to include the collective wisdom of those around you by encouraging discussion and avoiding argument.

Today's the day!

THE CRITICAL ELEMENT

Every endeavor in our lives—be it personal or professional—has one or more critical elements. A critical element of any venture is the unique piece of the puzzle that everything else relies upon. I regularly have people call, write, or stop by my office to offer me all types of "amazing" business opportunities. Most of these "amazing" business opportunities have one critical element that has been eliminated or overlooked. For example, someone might call up and explain how, for a modest investment, I can buy into a huge percentage of their operation involving a goose that lays golden eggs. These eggs are worth thousands of dollars, and we're all going to be rich.

This promoter, salesperson, or would-be entrepreneur wants to talk about everything but the critical element. He will invariably explain how they have figured the cost of feeding the goose, caring for the goose, and protecting the goose, as well as all details surrounding shipping the golden eggs to market. The one critical element they do not want to discuss is, quite simply: Does this goose really lay golden eggs?

In the vast majority of ventures proposed to you, if you will identify and probe the critical element as quickly as possible, you will save yourself a lot of time, money, and headaches. When it's all said and done, there's always more said than done, and people don't like to discuss the critical element because they want to live in a fairy-tale land instead of in reality. Unfortunately, you and I have to live our lives in reality. If other people want to be delusional, there's absolutely no reason for us to join them.

I have always felt that the Ten Commandments are hard enough to live by, but for some reason, years ago in one of my books, I wrote what I call Stovall's Eleventh Commandment, which simply states: Thou shalt not kid thyself. Or to state it more eloquently, quoting Mr. Shakespeare, "To thine own self be true."

Any business opportunity, investment, or venture of any type is only as strong as its weakest link. Identify it as quickly as possible, and if it holds up and proves to be valid, you can proceed full steam ahead. If not, don't waste your time in fairy-tale land.

My team here at Narrative Television Network tries to employ a principle we call accelerating your point of failure. The only thing worse than failing today is failing a year from now. Test everything carefully, locate and examine the critical element, and either cash in or move on.

As you go through your day today, focus on every critical element in your life and maximize your opportunities.

Today's the day!

HARD WORK AND FATIGUE

Many of us come home after a hard day's work feeling fatigued and worn out. If asked, we would honestly respond that the hard work has caused our weariness. In reality, hard work can be exhilarating, while frustration, delays, conflict, and unproductiveness wear us out and create fatigue.

As a professional speaker at conventions and arena events, I spend quite a bit of time traveling through airports around the world. People often comment on how tiring travel can be. The travel, itself, is not really all that tiring. It's the delays, frustration, long lines, and lack of coordination that often creates the tired and weary traveler.

Too many people confuse activity with productivity. Activity is tiring. Productivity is invigorating as you can observe the progress you have made toward your goal. Just because you're busy and tired does not necessarily mean you're getting anything done. The hamster in the cage running furiously on the spinning wheel is creating a lot of activity and no productivity. It is running a great distance without making any progress.

There are several things you can do to avoid the time-wasters and fatigue-creators in your life.

1. Have a daily list of priorities you want to accomplish. Order them from the most important to the least so if you run out of day before you run out of list, you've accomplished the maximum possible for your efforts.

2. Try to avoid trivia, interruptions, junk mail, and unsolicited calls. This is much harder than it sounds as there are countless people wanting to make their priorities and problems your focus for the day.

3. Schedule brief breaks during the day. Take a walk, read a magazine, or call a friend. Five minutes of distraction and recreation

can make all the difference. Sometimes it's easier to get an hour's worth of work done in fifty-five minutes than in a full hour.

4. Get in the practice of relegating everything on your list to one of three outcomes: do it, move it, or scratch it. When you close the book on today's activities, everything on your list should be completed, rescheduled for another day, or determined to be so insignificant as not to be pursued.

You are the most important commodity in your business and personal life. We allow people to waste our time, energy, and focus while we would never allow them to steal our money or resources.

As you go through your day today, focus on priorities and avoid the time-wasters and fatigue-creators.

Today's the day!

CUSTOMER CONSERVATION

Progress in business can be defined as getting new customers for your products and services. A lot goes into this activity, but—at the end of the day—this is how we measure growth. Other activities either support this growth or maintain the business we currently have. Satisfied customers are the key to life and success.

People in business pay huge amounts of money and go through amazing efforts to get lists or databases of potential customers. You might be surprised to know that you currently have free and easy access to one of the most amazing and underutilized customer lists in the world. If you will go to your computer, your filing cabinet, or your Rolodex, you will find untold numbers of former customers, underserved customers, or customers who are expanding their needs.

These people need to hear from you on a regular basis. There is a great old vaudeville joke that asks the question, "When should you tell your wife you love her?" The answer is, "Before someone else does." This is also true of your customers and former customers.

Your current customers should hear from you regularly, and you should explore the following things with them:

1. How do they feel about your products and services?
2. How can you better serve them?
3. What are their plans in the future that could increase your level of service to them?
4. What other companies and individuals do they know who should be prospects for your products or services?

Next, you need to go to that dreaded list of people who are former customers. In most cases, you won't be able to remember why they stopped doing business with you. The ironic thing is, your former customers probably don't remember why they quit doing business with you, either. You need to contact them and discuss the following:

1. They were a valued customer with whom you would like to reestablish a relationship.
2. If either of you are aware why the relationship ceased, solve the problem.
3. Determine how their business has changed or their needs may have expanded since you did business with them.
4. Ask them what you can do to regain their trust and build on the relationship.

Unfortunately, whether it's a personal or professional relationship, too often we will do more to get the relationship than we will do to keep it. Remember, you need always to be in a sales, marketing, and service mode with everyone you do business with. If you're not in this mode, you can rest assured that your competition will be.

As you go through your day today, value and expand on your current customer relationships and repair and restore your former ones.

Today's the day!

VOLTAIRE'S GARDENING TIPS

I f you're like most people, you have little or no knowledge of Voltaire other than dim memories from high school or college world-history classes. Voltaire was an eighteenth-century French philosopher. He is known for deep thought and practical advice on living. I would like to think that if Voltaire were alive today, he might write a column something like this one, but I probably flatter myself.

In a recent auction in Paris, the highest price ever paid was for a handwritten letter. It was a letter that Voltaire had written to a friend and colleague almost three hundred years ago. Apparently, the two were corresponding about issues of the day, politics, and critiques of some of their contemporaries. Then Voltaire wrote a line that should speak to us today. In fact, it would almost be worth the $1 million paid for the letter at auction to buy it and make sure that every political, business, religious, and social leader read Voltaire's words.

In the midst of the letter to his friend, Voltaire gave some gardening advice that can improve all of our lives, both personally and professionally. Voltaire said, "Hoe in your own garden."

We exist in a society, work in businesses, and live in families that have a number of visible weeds. We all collectively must deal with these weeds, but before we do or at least as we do, it's important that we hoe in our own garden. Very few of us could stand up to the light of criticism that we regularly shine on others. We judge others harshly in black-and-white terms but view ourselves through a mirror covered by smoke and muted tones. We understand our own intentions but only understand the actions of others; therefore, in the court of our own mind, we are great defense attorneys.

This is not to say that as a citizen, a business person, or a family member, we should not bring things to light that can improve the world.

But remember, all change, all development, and all improvement begins with us. If we will but heed Voltaire's admonition and "hoe in our own garden," I think we will find the weeds to be significant and plentiful to the extent that we have abundant matters to occupy our attentions.

As you go through your day today, look for ways to improve the world around you. Begin each improvement with the advice of Voltaire and "hoe in your own garden."

Today's the day!

JUST-RIGHT MANAGEMENT

Management is among the most used and least understood terms in our world today. Management ranges from an extreme of micromanagement to the opposite end of the spectrum, which is virtually no management.

When it's all said and done, all we can really manage is ourselves. The activities we call management, coaching, and oversight are nothing more than helping other people manage themselves and their activities. It should be thought of much like the three bears eating their porridge. You don't want the management too hot, because it burns everyone out. You don't want it too cold, because there's no motivation and unity. Instead, you want the management to be just right.

I recently read a biography of John D. Rockefeller. Apparently Rockefeller was asked by a reporter, "How much are you worth?" Rockefeller's response is quite telling with respect to just-right management. Rockefeller responded, "I don't know the exact number, and my accountants tell me that it would cost $10 million to determine the exact number, so all I can say is, I'm worth $10 million more than I would be if I could answer that question."

Most organizations perform tasks at an acceptable or even a high level. Unfortunately, too often they are doing a good job of performing the wrong task. If you believe the business rule, as I do, that we tend to improve the things we measure, it's very important to be sure we measure the right things and measure them accurately.

I began my business career as an investment broker, or better stated, a salesperson. I had a sales manager who required me to fill out voluminous call sheets and reports on each contact I made. While this may work in some contexts, I was so internally motivated to build my business that I found the three-hour daily drudge of doing this management paperwork to be totally deflating.

When you micromanage something or someone, you risk sending out the message, "I don't trust you." When you undermanage or mismanage, you send out the message, "I place little or no value in what you are doing." If you want to know the better way to manage people, start by simply asking them. This will give you some clarity in the process and give you permission to begin oversight. Quit thinking in terms of bossing people, and start thinking in terms of helping people.

As you go through your day today, find people and situations where you can begin adjusting management until it's just right.

Today's the day!

Ad of us work with other people. Even if you work alone from your home, you are dependent upon contractors, couriers, and service providers. If you work in an office setting, you interact with people constantly. Many times, success and failure will be determined by how well we work with those around us.

Each of us should start every day with an actual list of things to be accomplished. By the end of the day, everything on the list should be completed, moved to another day, or delegated to someone else. Delegation is potentially the biggest breakdown in business today. Please remember: Delegated is not "done." Just because you've handed it off doesn't mean the task is completed. Follow-up and follow-through are critical. This follow-up and follow-through may take the form of checking on that person to whom you have delegated a task several days, weeks, or months later. It may also take the form of expecting them to follow up with you as the last step of the task you're delegating, but you still must put it on your calendar to expect their follow-up.

I work with the most competent team of professionals I have ever met. Having said that, everything in our office is checked and double-checked systematically. If you're doing something that is not important enough to have it checked or confirmed, you need to find something more important to do.

I have flown well over one million miles commercially, and in every plane I board, there are at least two people totally qualified to fly that aircraft. From time to time for certain events I travel in a private plane. On each occasion, I make certain there is a qualified pilot and copilot. On the private plane, I sit just a few feet behind the cockpit, so I can hear everything going on up there. It's interesting to note that most of the time the two pilots are communicating, they are cross-checking each other. This is not because they don't trust the other's competency. It's because a mistake means life or death. Anything worth doing is worth doing to the best of your ability and having another qualified person double-check.

As you go through your day today, delegate everything you can, do everything you can't, and have it all checked.

Today's the day!

P. T. Barnum will forever be known as one of the greatest showmen of all time. He was renowned for his marketing and promotional ability. If you read much about his life, you will find that most stories about Barnum present him as an outrageous, over-the-top wild man. You may be surprised to know that recently in studying the life of Barnum, I read a direct quote from him that is probably the best advice on money, balance, and life in general that I have ever heard. Barnum said, "Money is a terrible master but an excellent servant."

Nothing will take the place of money in the things that money does. Money will not solve any problems, but it will certainly cure some symptoms. On the other hand, if you will list all of the things you treasure most—such as the love of your family, the esteem of your friends, the treasure of good health, or the freedom to pursue your life on your own terms—you will quickly realize that money is not a part of the equation.

When you look at the national statistics on household net worth, it is alarming. We have the highest debt-to-income ratio we have had since the 1930s. The difference between now and the 1930s is that we enjoy a good economy, low inflation, and high employment rather than suffering the terrible conditions of the Great Depression. People today are in a mad rush to buy things they don't need with money they don't have to impress people who don't care.

The health of the world's economy or the national economy really doesn't matter nearly as much as the health of your personal economy. Some of the greatest fortunes were built during the Depression, and many people have lived in poverty during times of wealth and prosperity. The ominous outlook rests on the question that if people are barely keeping their heads above water now, what are they going to do when (not if) the economy takes one of its natural downturns?

Here are a few personal financial checkup tips.

1. Determine how many months you could survive financially without incurring any more debt if all your income were shut off today. If it's not a minimum of six months, you need to establish more liquid reserves.

2. Eliminate consumer debt as a regular part of your monthly cycle. If you can't pay for it now, you probably won't be able to pay for it later with interest.

3. Look into the future and start planning, saving, and investing for upcoming expenses. College tuition, home repairs, health challenges, and retirement should not catch you by surprise.

As you go through your day today, make money your slave, not your master.

Today's the day!

LESSONS FROM TARZAN

If, like me, you grew up as a fan of the Edgar Rice Burroughs Tarzan books or the *Tarzan* TV show and movies, you may be aware of a very important principle that you may not have applied to your life and your business.

Tarzan had a very unique and effective way of transporting himself through the jungle. He, of course, would swing from vine to vine through the treetops until he arrived at his destination. If you will think back and remember this process, you will remember that Tarzan never let go of one vine until he had the next chosen or firmly in hand. Too often in our personal or professional lives, we look at the next big decision or the next big event, but we fail to look beyond the very next thing into the future to see how everything fits together in order to get us from where we are to where we want to be.

Great chess players think many moves ahead. They plan, they anticipate, and they strategize. Interviews of over-the-road truck drivers who have driven over a million accident-free miles reveal that successful drivers look far into the distance and anticipate what will be coming at them down the road.

In order to learn and benefit from Tarzan's lesson, you must first have, firmly in your mind, a clear picture of where you want to end up. If you don't know where you're going, any vine or no vine at all will do. A road map is a useful tool only for people who have a clear understanding of two details. First, they know exactly where they are; and second, they know where they want to be. If a clear understanding of either of these points is missing, the map is entirely useless. Success is always simple, but never easy. If you know where you want to go, the route is not hard to find, but it may be hard to follow.

One of the advantages you and I have over Tarzan is the fact that most of us can follow in the footsteps of successful people who have gone before us. The high road to success is, indeed, the "road less traveled," but it has been traveled and offers a clearly delineated path for those who want to put one foot in front of the other, look into the distance, plan, anticipate, dream, and succeed.

As you go through your day today, remember that the right decision can only be made in light of your entire journey.

Today's the day!

PAY ATTENTION

This morning, I heard about an exceptional young man who graduated from high school this year. He achieved a perfect score on both of the national college entrance exams. When asked how he accomplished this or what advice he would give to other students, he offered a brief but poignant statement. "Pay attention." While this may seem simple, it's important to remember that all great and enduring truths are inevitably simple. We don't fail because we don't know what to do; we fail because we don't do what we know.

The simple admonition to pay attention is deeper than you might first imagine. All of us pay attention. Many of us too often pay attention to the wrong things.

Several years ago, I was the keynote speaker for a major business convention held on an island in the Caribbean. After my presentation, the promoters of the event had arranged for two famous Las Vegas magicians to perform. As I was still backstage following my speech, I had an opportunity to meet and talk with these magicians. I asked the obvious question that most of you would ask: "How do you make a four-hundred-pound tiger disappear right before the eyes of thousands of people who are on the edge of their seats paying attention?" One of the magicians laughed and responded, "Fortunately for us, they are all paying attention to the right thing at the wrong time and the wrong thing at the right time." The two magicians assured me that if they told everyone the magic secret before their performance, no one in the arena could fail to observe how the illusion is performed.

So, as we're striving to pay attention, it is critical that we pay attention to the right things. While being fooled during an entertaining Las Vegas magic show may be great, being fooled while looking at the wrong things in our personal and professional lives can be disastrous.

I recently heard about a survey conducted nationally among high school seniors. While over 90 percent of these young people could name three members of the Simpson family from the popular TV show, less than 10 percent of them could name three supreme court justices. Over a third of them could not name our vice president; therefore, it is obvious that these young people are definitely paying attention. The question that will determine success and failure remains: What are they paying attention to?

As you go through your day today, determine what is important to you and pay attention to it. Tune out everything else.

Today's the day!

A braham Lincoln gave the world the sentiment that if honesty were not pursued because it is simply the right thing to do, it should at least be pursued as the quickest way to succeed.

There is no contract that can ever fully protect you from a dishonest person, and there is no dispute or challenge that cannot be overcome between honest people. Honesty is not simply the absence of a lie but communicating all the information that people are entitled to and that they rely on. Unfortunately, some of our leaders have demonstrated you can communicate a lie while technically telling the truth, or at least not perjuring yourself legally.

Whether it's President Clinton or O. J. Simpson, the lack of a clear and complete truth will taint you forever. President Clinton is a respected leader that has many accomplishments to his credit. He came from an obscure town in a small state and became arguably the most powerful man in the world. O. J. Simpson overcame many challenges in his life to become the very best at his chosen profession of football. Both of these gentlemen are entitled to respect for their accomplishments; however, it's very difficult to think of them without the taint of their misdeeds and dishonesty following closely behind.

It takes a lifetime to build a solid reputation and a moment to damage it. Unfortunately, in our litigious, media-driven world, people can be known for their single worst deed instead of a lifetime of good deeds.

Think of all the people in the world whom you trust totally. I don't mean that they won't steal your wallet when you're not looking or purposely miscount the change for a ten-dollar bill. I mean people who communicate clearly and mean what they say just as they say what they mean. If you can think of more than a handful of people who you consider to be totally honest, you've probably not set the standard high enough when you think of honesty.

The purpose of honest communication is to communicate the intent and the reality between everyone involved. Too many people use communication for an opportunity to spin, oversell, or hype the situation as they wish it were instead of how it really is.

When you're communicating a deal, an offer, or an opportunity to someone, you must be able to say in your own mind, "If they knew what I knew, they would be as excited about this as I am." If anything more or less needs to be added, this is probably not a positive deal that is based on total honesty.

As you go through your day today, recommit yourself to being totally clear and totally honest in every situation. It's the right thing to do and the best way to succeed.

Today's the day!

PERSONAL OPINION POLL

We spend an inordinate amount of time, effort, energy, and money to impress people with whom we come in contact. Unfortunately, most of these people don't care about us and are not impressed with our car, clothes, or other paraphernalia that we somehow feel to be imperative.

In the final analysis, the only opinion of us that really matters is the one we have of ourselves. Our thoughts, ambitions, and expectations are what define us as people. We have the ability to craft and change these with the force of our will.

Recently, a valued friend and colleague shared with me some of his personal and professional affirmations. These statements are how he chooses to view himself. He has, in effect, taken his own self-opinion poll and decided who he is and how his life should be ordered. I got his permission to share some of his life statements with you.

Who Am I?

I love life and take no day or opportunity for granted.

I am devoted to waking up early each day. I do so revived, full of energy, psyched to work out and seize the day.

I love my family. Everything I do is revolved around my commitment to our well-being.

I am an extremely lucky man. The harder I work the luckier I get. I have unrelenting energy and never stop working toward the goals that are important to me.

I am an incredible adviser. I love to coach others to maximize their wealth and the choices wealth creates.

I think only the best, work with only the best, and expect only the best for myself and those I serve.

I am an exceptional business partner. I contribute and compromise for the betterment of the firm and our collective futures.

I am a great inspiration to my family, clients, coworkers, and friends. I am as enthusiastic about the success of others as I am about my own.

I am an optimist even when everybody else is not. I learn from and then forget about mistakes of the past and press on toward the better opportunities of present and future.

I am honest and moral. I always do what's in the best interest of others.

I am physically, fiscally, and emotionally sound! I am in constant pursuit to improve, grow, and make life better.

I believe in what I say. I say what I will do. I do what I say.

I believe these statements for they are fact.

This is who I am!

I want to thank my friend and colleague for a glimpse into his life and who he chooses to be.

As you go through your day today, remember, your life is a choice. Choose wisely.

Today's the day!

I f you are traveling on an extended road trip along a divided highway, you see two sets of cars. There are the cars on your side of the road going the same direction that you are, and there are those on the opposite side of the road going the other way. If you were to stop at a rest stop to inquire about weather or road conditions ahead, you would not want to ask those traveling the same way as you. Instead, you would want to ask those traveling in the opposite direction, because they have already been where you are going.

This is a major key to success in life. Too many people ask opinions of others who have not yet been where they wish to go. This makes absolutely no sense, but it happens every day.

My mentor in the television business has been Ted Turner. Mr. Turner, over the years, has given us very valuable advice, and while we rarely seek his opinion, it is very valuable to us because in our industry he has gone where everybody wants to go.

As an author and a platform speaker, my mentor is Dr. Denis Waitley. He has advised me many times and has kept me from wasting much time, effort, and energy. The reality is that he already has been for many years where I wish to go. When I asked Dr. Waitley why he was willing to take his valuable time to mentor me, he told me that, years ago, Earl Nightingale had mentored him, and it had made all the difference in his career. He went on to tell me that in the last days of his life, Mr. Nightingale implored Dr. Waitley to find someone whom he could mentor. I am very fortunate that Dr. Waitley chose me.

In the past several years, I have had the privilege of mentoring other people—some for a brief period of time, others over several years. Initially, I thought that this would just be my way of giving back the many benefits I had received from Mr. Turner and Dr. Waitley. Instead, I have found it to be a wonderful learning experience for me.

It reinforces many of the principles I have learned from others and causes me to rethink how I am conducting my life and my business.

When we learn, knowledge has been imparted. When we teach others, it has been transferred. But the magic of mentoring happens when we teach others to teach. Then and only then does the knowledge become the property of everyone who can benefit from learning, teaching, and sharing.

Today's the day!

It is important to realize that success is success and failure is failure in any and every endeavor of life. It is easy to get caught up in the notion that the grass is greener on the other side of the fence. This type of thinking tells us that "If I would just switch jobs, switch careers, move to a different city ... I would be successful."

While I am a big advocate of pursuing your passion and would be the first to tell you to make a change if it involves pursuing your passion, there are times when the other path seems more inviting. Even when you are on your life's course pursuing your destiny, there will be times that you deal with frustrating issues and difficult situations. At these times, it is important to avoid jumping off the right track and moving onto some insignificant and irrelevant tangent.

Those people who are successful in every area of life enjoy a wonderful existence. Those people who are failing suffer a miserable existence no matter what course they are pursuing. There is no good place to fail or bad place to succeed.

I have an acquaintance who has changed careers every twelve to eighteen months throughout his adult life. It's not because he is seeking his ultimate destiny, but, instead, he is looking for an easier course. Be it success, money, or happiness, I have never found nor spoken with anyone who has found the easy road to getting everything wanted out of life. Success is not easy, nor is it immediate, but it is worth working and waiting for.

If you are seeking to reach a certain elevation in your life and you begin climbing the mountain before you, when it gets rough and steep, it is tempting to look across the valley at what appears to be the nice, gentle incline of another mountain. Those who abandon their current mountain, journey through the valley, and begin climbing the opposite peak will discover steep and rocky paths up that mountain as well. It is ironic, because when they look back across the valley to the peak where they began their climb, it will appear to be a smooth, easy, unencumbered climb to the top.

Be resolved to stay the course through the difficult times, and before you know it, you will be standing on the summit.

Today's the day!

THE SLEEPING GIANT

Recently during a speaking engagement in Hawaii, I had the privilege of touring Pearl Harbor and the USS *Arizona* Memorial. It is a moving experience that I would recommend to anyone who has the opportunity to take advantage of it. From time to time, it is good to be reminded that freedom comes at a very high price.

As I was doing a bit of research about World War II and the Pearl Harbor attack, I came across the famous quote from Admiral Isoroku Yamamoto. After the Japanese attack on the United States on December 7, 1941, he said, "I fear all we have done is to awaken a sleeping giant." The surprise attack, while devastating to our navy, did, indeed, awaken the people of the United States and fill us with a tremendous resolve. Often in our lives, adversity or challenge can awaken the sleeping giant within us as individuals. I have heard it said that anything that does not destroy us serves to make us even stronger.

There are many lessons to be taken away from the Pearl Harbor experience. I was struck by the fact that many of those touring the memorial on the same day I did were Japanese nationals. There is no animosity left, only the futility of war and the lessons to be learned.

I believe that there is a giant within each of us that, when awakened, can perform at a level we have not yet even imagined. Think about where you are in your life and your career. Ask yourself what you could do if you were forced to, and then ask yourself why you are not performing at that level right now.

It could be argued that, had the United States performed before the Pearl Harbor attack as we performed after the attack, it is possible that war could have been avoided altogether. One of the lessons of Pearl Harbor is that effort expended before a crisis is much more valuable than that expended after a crisis.

Think about the giant within you and awaken it yourself. Don't wait on a disaster to perform at your best.

Today's the day!

More professional and personal conflicts arise from unfulfilled expectations than anything else. Conflicts, arguments, and disagreements do, indeed, exist; however, most of them can be overcome if we learn to manage our expectations and those of others.

Expectationville is a place where we mentally go when we are planning and organizing other people's lives. It's great to have expectations for ourselves, but when we place them on other people, we are on thin ice. The only way to avoid experiencing a very unpleasant visit to Expectationville is to take a brief detour through Communication Land.

When we place our expectations on other people—whether we realize it or not—we have set up a black-and-white, right-and-wrong situation. Not only do they have to perform a certain task, but in our mind, they have to perform it the way we visualized it during our trip to Expectationville. If, indeed, we are going to set up these kinds of rigid boundaries for other people, the least we can do is to let them know where the boundary lines are located. This is accomplished when we take our trip through Communication Land.

Have you ever planned a trip with someone else and realized early in the planning or during the trip itself that the two of you are simply "not on the same page"? This doesn't necessarily make the other person right or wrong, it simply makes their plans different from your expectations. If you have planned a trip and you know your flight leaves at a certain time, you may have communicated the departure time to your traveling companion; however, in your mind, you have been spending some time in Expectationville creating boundaries. These boundaries may say, "If the flight's at eight in the morning, we will want to be at the airport at six; therefore, we need to leave at five thirty." This is all clear in your mind, because everything is neat and orderly in Expectationville, but if you and your traveling companion have not spent any time in Communication Land, they may be thinking, "If the flight's at eight, we can leave for the airport at six thirty."

Either schedule might work quite well; however, you will find yourself frustrated and disappointed because your traveling companion is "late." Because of your uncommunicated expectations, you may think your traveling companion is rude, insensitive, and habitually late. They, sensing your frustration, will wonder why you have a bad attitude and what might be your problem. Today, try to eliminate expectations you have of others or commit to communicate those expectations.

Today's the day!

The goal of being everything to everyone all the time is nothing more than an elusive myth. The statement "You can't please all the people all the time" is true. We have all heard the campaign promises that we can lower taxes, increase spending, stop all wars, and have peace on earth and good will toward men. We discount these statements when they are made by politicians in the heat of a campaign, but we need to learn that trying to please everyone in our own lives will result in pleasing no one—most importantly, ourselves.

The only opinion that really matters is the one we have of ourselves. We spend far too much time trying to impress those around us and far too little trying to satisfy our own dreams and desires.

In my travels making corporate speeches, I often have the opportunity to meet one-on-one with executives and sales people. It amazes me how many people are often committing their time, effort, and energy to reaching other people's goals. Whether it's losing weight, finding financial success, or reaching personal achievements, we must take ownership of the objectives if we are to succeed. Simply because someone else thinks you should change your life does not necessarily signal that this is a goal you should embrace as well. Goals are hard enough to reach when they are our own. They are impossible to reach when they belong to someone else.

We have all seen average sales achievers—seemingly overnight—turn into top-level performers. More often than not, this change comes when they internalize a goal and take possession of it. When those salespeople decide that their boss's quotas are something they want to strive for, they become real and achievable. Focus on your own goals and objectives, not those that friends, family, or society try to impose upon you.

It's not enough just to win. To have long-term satisfaction, you must win at the right game. Today, commit yourself to really examining the goals and objectives you seek in every area of your life. Make sure they are your own.

Today's the day!

EXPERIENCE IS A TEACHER

If you were to list all of the things you know—that you believe and you are willing to act upon—chances are this knowledge has come from an experience. Not all experiences result in corresponding knowledge of course. You have met people who suffer the same negative experience time after time but, somehow, do not learn the corresponding lesson that will enable them to avoid negative experiences in the future. Ignorant people will walk out into the rain day after day after day lamenting the fact that they are getting wet.

On the other hand, there are other certain enlightened or highly developed people who can learn a life lesson from someone else's experience. These people exhibit a quality we would call wisdom. They do not have to suffer through a difficulty in order to benefit from a learning experience. Knowledgeable people will walk out into the rain once or twice and then learn to check first and take an umbrella when appropriate. Wise people can observe others who are coming in from the elements and determine that they need to prepare for the rain without actually getting wet themselves.

If we do, indeed, know what we know through experiences, whether our own or those of others, we need to constantly ask ourselves: What experiences have we had or are we having that we need to learn from? What can we learn from observing the mistakes of others? Life will continue to rain upon you unless or until you learn the appropriate lesson. There are much more subtle experiences, both good and bad, that can result in fabulous lessons. We must constantly look for them.

Each time something good happens, ask yourself: What can I do to repeat that? Each time something bad happens, ask yourself: How can I avoid that in the future? When you see those around you succeeding in a way you find significant, ask yourself: How can I mirror that kind of success? When you see people around you suffering as a result of their own poor decisions, ask yourself: How can I learn that lesson without going through that challenge? In doing so, we can move from ignorance to knowledge, and—hopefully—to wisdom.

Today's the day!

SELF-INDUCED STRESS

S cience is continuing to prove that stress is at the root of many diseases and much pain and suffering. Our fast-paced lives and the uncertainty that surrounds us all in our personal and professional lives creates a high level of stress for everyone, but there is an additional stress that I believe robs people from finding happiness and reaching their potential. This we could call self-induced stress.

Stress does not come from hard work but, instead, from the frustration of unfulfilled potential and unproductive time or effort. My business requires me to do quite a bit of traveling via the airlines. Since the tragedy of September 11, this has, of course, become much more difficult and—for many people—much more stressful. During my last trip, I had to catch a flight out of my hometown, Tulsa, Oklahoma, and make a connection in Dallas in order to catch a plane to New Orleans in order to make a speech at an arena event.

For many speakers, such trips are very stressful. You are contractually bound to be at a certain place at a certain time with great financial rewards or penalties hanging in the balance. Many speakers or celebrities have a list of horror stories from their time on the road. In order to avoid as much stress as possible, we have undertaken a policy of booking flights well in advance of the deadline with several backup flights in case there are mechanical or weather problems. I have sat on many airplanes with people around me experiencing high levels of stress simply because they failed to plan ahead. I am certainly not better than these individuals. I have simply learned from my own mistakes.

As you go through your day today, pay special attention to the times you are feeling stressed. Ask the following questions: What is causing this stress? Is the stressful feeling valid? And is there anything I could have done in advance to avoid this stressful situation? You will find yourself much happier, more productive, and far less stressed.

Today's the day!

MONEY MYTHS

Money is probably the most misunderstood commodity in the history of humanity. While it is not the most important thing in life, nothing can take the place of money in the things that money does. If we are to understand money and use it properly, we must dispel the old and deeply ingrained money myths:

1. *Money will make you happy.* All one need do to prove this to be false is to look at the entertainment news and see how much heartbreak, divorce, and suicide play a part in the lives of the rich and famous. Money will certainly not make you happy, but neither will poverty. It is important to have just enough money to reach all of the goals and dreams we have.

2. *Some people are lucky when it comes to money.* Only those who work in a mint make money. The rest of us earn money. Money is earned by labor or by money earning additional money. Even if you hear about someone who has been given money, always remember someone earned that money, or it was derived via investment. If you want to have more money, learn how to create more value in the lives of others, and the money will follow.

3. *Money is evil.* Money is absolutely neutral. It is not good or bad. Like a gun, knife, or any other tool, it can be used to any end. The most horrible atrocities and the most wonderful blessings ever known have been facilitated by money.

4. *Average people cannot get ahead.* There are more millionaires being created today than ever before. They are not born millionaires. They simply find a way to create enough value in the lives of people so that they are rewarded financially. Compound interest should be known globally as the Eighth Wonder of the World. Most people understand exchanging their time and effort for money. What millionaires understand is that money will begat

more money if it is saved and invested wisely. No one ever borrowed their way to financial independence. You must get on the positive side of the compound interest wave.

Examine your financial goals and the vehicles you are using to reach them. Take all of the emotion out of the money game, and use it as a tool. Always remember to love people and use money. If you get this backward, you will be destined to fail no matter how much you have.

Today's the day!

The Prominence of Problems

hat do Benjamin Franklin, Adolf Hitler, Winston Churchill, Thomas Edison, William Shakespeare, Osama bin Laden, and every other historical or famous person you have ever heard of have in common? Every famous or infamous person that has come to historical prominence is known for either solving or creating problems.

When you think of the people you know in your personal or professional circles, you probably think of them in terms of whether they solve or create problems. All human endeavor hinges on the simple task of solving or creating problems. Great ideas are nothing more or less than the solutions to problems. The greater the problem, the greater the idea that solves it.

Great businesses are nothing more than the solving of other people's problems. Successful enterprises continue to grow and thrive based on how well and to what extent they solve problems. Income is based on the extent of the problem that you solve and how well you solve it.

A garbage collector solves a real problem. If you don't think so, just let them miss your house for a few weeks, and the problem will become readily apparent. Brain surgeons solve a quite different problem. You can learn to be a garbage collector in a few weeks, but in order to be a brain surgeon you must invest many years. The problem that a brain surgeon solves is, quite literally, life and death; therefore, a good brain surgeon will earn many multiples of the income of a garbage collector.

We have been trained since we were children to avoid problems. We have also been trained to honor and respect people who, down through the years, have solved problems. These two ideas are at odds with one another. In order to be successful, we cannot avoid problems.

We must get out in front of the herd, find the problems, and solve them—not only for ourselves but for everyone else.

Remember: Your friends, your family, and history itself will not remember you for the problems you avoid. They will remember you for either the problems you create or those you solve, making the world a better place to live.

As you go through your day today, look upon problems not as an obstacle to avoid but as an opportunity to seize and harvest. You will improve your life and the lives of many people around you.

Today's the day!

ADVICE ON FAILURE

It is difficult to turn on your television or radio without being confronted by some supposed expert telling you how to be successful in your personal or professional life. Virtually every newspaper, magazine, or publication—including the one you're reading now—contains "tips for this" or "steps to that." I am a big proponent of getting advice on success from successful people. The challenge is in determining who is truly successful and who is trying to become successful by selling you advice.

While you are seeking personal or professional advice on success, don't forget to get some good advice on failure. In every situation, and with every person we meet, we can identify things we want and things we don't want in our own lives. Often, learning why people who have failed did so can be as instructive as advice on success. I believe that success, happiness, and prosperity are the natural order of things. What we need to do to enjoy the good things in life is to remove and eliminate the failure.

It's as Michelangelo said when asked how he could create magnificent art out of a raw block of marble. He replied that all he need do is simply remove any marble that is not art, and that which remains must be a masterpiece.

I have a unique friend who recently lost over $1 billion. We have had a number of discussions that have taught me a great deal. First, I was able to learn how my friend made $1 billion, and second, I was additionally able to learn how he lost an incredible fortune. When you think about it, my friend has more to teach than the average billionaire you might run across. The average billionaire might know how to create wealth, but they may not have learned how to avoid losing wealth.

The only thing one need do to have a great idea is to go through life day to day and wait for something bad to happen. Then ask the question, "How could I have avoided that?" The answer to the question will invariably be a great and creative idea. The only thing one need do to create a great opportunity or business is to ask oneself, "How can I help other people avoid their problems?" The answer to this question will result in a great and profitable venture.

As you go through your day today, learn lessons from success, but don't overlook the magic knowledge to be gained from failure.

Today's the day!

ABOUT THE AUTHOR

Jim Stovall has overcome the challenges of blindness to become a national Olympic weightlifting champion, a successful investment broker and entrepreneur, and a highly sought-after platform speaker. He is cofounder and president of the Narrative Television Network, which makes movies and television accessible for our nation's 13 million blind and visually impaired people and their families. Although the network originally was designed for blind and visually impaired people, over 60 percent of NTN's nationwide audience is made up of fully sighted people who simply enjoy the programming.

Jim Stovall hosts the network's talk show, *NTN Showcase*. His guests have included Katharine Hepburn, Jack Lemmon, Carol Channing, Steve Allen, and Eddie Albert, as well as many others. The Narrative Television Network has received an Emmy Award and an International Film and Video Award among its many industry honors.

NTN has grown to include more than 1,200 cable systems and broadcast stations, reaching over 35 million homes in the United States, and NTN is shown in eleven foreign countries. NTN programming is also presented via the Internet at NarrativeTV.com, serving millions of people around the world.

Jim Stovall joined the ranks of Walt Disney, Orson Welles, and four United States presidents when he was selected as one of the Ten Outstanding Young Americans by the US Junior Chamber of Commerce. He has appeared on *Good Morning America* and CNN, and has been featured in *Reader's Digest, TV Guide,* and *Time* magazine. He is the author of previous books including *You Don't Have to Be Blind to See, Success Secrets of Super Achievers, The Way I See the World,* and *The Ultimate Gift.* The President's Committee on Equal

Opportunity selected Jim Stovall as the 1997 Entrepreneur of the Year. In 2000, Jim Stovall was selected as the International Humanitarian of the Year, joining Jimmy Carter, Nancy Reagan, and Mother Teresa. He can be reached at 918-627-1000.